# ENDORSEMENTS

"Anyone who thinks that one can't be gay and Christian MUST READ *God's Gay Agenda*. I found this book inspiring, entertaining, enlightening and a joy to read."
—**Wayne Besen**, Founder, Truth Wins Out

"For anyone who takes the scripture seriously and struggles to reconcile or help other's reconcile their sexuality and spirituality, Sandra has provided an invaluable resource."
—**Rev. Michael S. Piazza**, retired Senior Pastor of the Cathedral of Hope and author of *Holy Homosexuals*.

"Sandra Turnbull has done an amazing job of telling the story of her search for God's agenda for her life as an openly lesbian pastor and of her gift of interpreting what Hebrew and Christian scripture says about homosexuality and same-gender marriage. This book is a must read."
—**Rev. Troy D. Perry**, Founder, Metropolitan Community Churches.

"The authors premise is true; unlike the insidious 'gay agenda' often referred to in conservative Christian literature God does have his own Gay Agenda of love, grace and equality."
—**Anthony Venn-Brown**, author of *Life Of Unlearning*.

# GOD'S GAY AGENDA

BY
## SANDRA TURNBULL

Kelly —
Great to hear from you again! I hope you enjoy the book. It is a calling for us to live with purpose.

Much love
ST

GP

*God's Gay Agenda*

Published by:

Glory Publishing

9812 Walnut St.

Bellflower, CA 90706

ISBN 978-0-9883863-0-3

# CONTENTS

# DEDICATION

This book is dedicated to all who may struggle with their sexual orientation and who seek to find their place in God. I pray that this book is Good News for you. I also wrote this book with families in mind. I pray for the restoration of families who have been torn apart because of a gay, lesbian, bisexual, or transgender family member.

I also dedicate this book to the Holy Spirit who allowed me to write it.

Finally, this book is dedicated to my Uncle Ted. I'm so glad you made it into the kingdom of heaven. Somehow the Lord connected us together during your last days of illness when you told me you had been following my "career." You came to your nieces' Church and gave your heart to the Lord that Sunday. I'm certain that it was just the assurance of your salvation that you were seeking. I dedicate this book to you, Uncle Ted, in the hope that others will not have to go through the hardships you endured.

# Acknowledgments

Thank you, Janet, for fulfilling the call to walk with me as we journey with Christ. You are my dream come true! You are also the most courageous person I know.

Thank you, Mom and Dad, for giving me such a rich heritage in God. It is because of the streams of my Christian heritage that I keep digging a well in a desert land.

A big thank you to Glory Tabernacle Christian Center, a wonderful Church that I am privileged to lead. You reveal the heart of Jesus in being an inclusive congregation. Thank you for being a catalyst for this new move of God's Spirit in the earth today. I am grateful to my elders and friends who have watched me grow and have kept me steady over the years.

Finally, thanks to Rev. Dr. Dusty Pruitt for training me, Rev. Don Eastman for encouraging me, and Rev. Freda Smith for sharing your dream of me in January 1996. I hope I have turned out to be "God's little fountain pen."

# INTRODUCTION

In January 1995, God called me into full-time Christian ministry. Up until then, I had always had a vague idea that God wanted to use me for His purposes. But, that day, I heard an audible voice call me to pastor a Church. This significant moment in my life took place at the Crystal Cathedral in Garden Grove, California. I was at the Crystal Cathedral on the invitation of my senior pastor who had invited me to attend the Robert Schuller Institute for Pastors. It was there that I heard, for the first time, Dr. Robert Schuller share personally the story of his call into Christian ministry.

It seems that Dr. Schuller grew up in a rather large family on a farm in Iowa. His uncle was a missionary to China and in those days he would send letters to his sister, Dr. Schuller's mother. These letters would be read to the entire family whenever they were received. It was in one of those letters that his uncle recounted that the missionaries to China had learned they would first have to meet the physical needs of the people before they could ever hope to meet their spiritual needs. These missionaries found out that if they fed the Chinese people with much needed rice, then their hearts were more open to receive the Gospel. This story was planted in young Schuller's mind to be used by the Lord much later in his life.

Later after graduating from a Dutch Reformed seminary and then being sent to serve a small congregation in Garden Grove, California, as pastor, Dr. Schuller began to seek the Lord for a way to reach the people in his area. He began to pray and ask God for a way into the hearts of the people. It was then that the Holy Spirit reminded him of what his uncle had learned so many years earlier in ministry to the Chinese people. Through prayer, God impressed upon Dr. Schuller that the *rice* for the people of Orange County, California, was self-esteem. He learned that when people are built up as God's creations and given respect, dignity, and love, then in turn their hearts are opened to discovering their self-worth purchased for them at the cross of Jesus Christ.

In the same way, when I was called to pastor Glory Tabernacle Christian Center, I began to seek God for understanding on what the *rice* was for the people I was sent to reach. As a congregation called to be inclusive of all people, I wanted to make inroads into the gay, lesbian, bisexual, and transgender communities along with their families and friends. Eventually, I sensed God impress upon my heart that the *rice* for this community was to know the purpose of God for setting them apart through their sexuality or uniqueness. If they could understand why God had created them so uniquely, then they would discover their special calling in God.

This book is a result of my seeking the Lord for insight specifically on homosexuality. I pray that the message of this book on God's calling and purpose is *rice* for all of God's special gay and lesbian children. I trust that revelation will come forth in the future concerning my brothers and sisters who are unique in other ways as far as sexuality or gender identity. This book in particular focuses on the truths concerning Jesus' words in Matthew 19:12 about eunuchs. What we will see is that natural-born eunuchs parallel what we know today to be gays and lesbians. Finally, since the ministry God has given me does reach out with God's love and embrace to all people, my prayer is that this book touches all of our hearts with His amazing love in a powerful way.

# 1

# GOD'S CALLING THE QUESTION

"Then the Lord answered Job out of the storm. He said: 'Who is this that darkens my counsel with words without knowledge? Brace yourself like a man; I will question you, and you shall answer me.'"
~Job 38:1-3

Over twenty-five years ago my life was turned upside down. I'm not referring to the day I accepted Christ because I experienced that joy when I was eight years old. It wasn't even the day that I was filled with the Holy Spirit either. I'm talking about the day I fell in love... that is, in love with a woman. My life exploded when as a young twenty-three-year-old I met my life partner, Janet.

It all happened in Amsterdam, Holland, where we met as part of Musicians for Missions, an offshoot of Youth With A Mission. I had never really been honest with myself about my sexuality since I had grown up in Church all my life. It was a "Don't Ask, Don't Tell" atmosphere, you could say. So, I learned to stuff emotions and to not look too closely at my feelings. I'm sure everyone else around me could read me, but I would not let myself be honest. By the time I got through Bible College and into Youth With A Mission, my sexuality was ready to break out of its confinement, whether religious or social. It was there in Amsterdam that one day I looked at the reflection of my face in a bathroom mirror and heard my lips say, "You are a lesbian." It was a self-defining moment.

It was too much for me to understand at the time and certainly too much for Youth With A Mission to cope with. Janet and I were separated from each other for forty-eight hours until I could be walked to the Amsterdam train station by an YWAM escort like a criminal—sent home to America. I knew somehow that her eyes were upon me then as I walked across the square to the station. And, sure enough, much later I found out that Janet had watched in sadness as I was removed from her life. We were banned from each other. We had fallen in love and the only way the Church knew how to deal with us was to separate us and try to quench the "sin." Or was it love?

For almost two years, I went through counseling and tried not to think of Janet. Yet, it seemed like my heart was beating at a whole new pace that was not in sync with my Christian upbringing. I went for Christian counseling through several ministries because of my "struggle" with homosexuality. I thought it was interesting that two of my counselors, I found out, were gay or lesbian themselves, but had just married heterosexually. It was all very confusing.

Finally, a day came when I guess my subconscious mind was able to get my conscious mind convinced that if I wrote Janet a Christmas card it was only because I wanted to be friends. I received a phone call from Janet months later after my Christmas card was forwarded from Holland, to Scotland, and from there to California, where Janet was now residing. I was delighted to see her again. Too delighted. My heart was once again becoming free. During this time, the lesbian in the mirror from Amsterdam was showing up and confronting my thinking.

As part of our courtship, Janet and I decided to study the issue of homosexuality and the Bible. We both were Christians. We both were in love with each other. Time didn't seem to dissipate love. Distance didn't seem to erase it. So, we thought we better find out what God had to say about our love and then make a decision about our future, whether together or apart.

I'll never forget the day we went to the Fuller Theological Seminary library in Pasadena, California and walked over to the aisle where the books on homosexuality were found. Janet grabbed several books and went and sat down at a table to begin reading. I stood in the aisle because my attention had been arrested by one book—*Jonathan Loved David* by Tom Horner. Tears ran down my cheeks as I stood in that library, glued to that book. I had always felt direction and comfort from the Holy Spirit, but it was amazing to read a book that only confirmed what I had sensed God speaking to me about in my heart. This was my first affirming book which detailed Jonathan and David's love for each other based upon the original Hebrew language and ancient culture. Things began to fall into place.

Since then, I have watched God move heaven and earth for Janet and me. We have been especially blessed to work side-by-side in establishing inclusive Churches in various nations. I also have a primary ministry of being the pastor of a dynamic Church in southern California where everyone is welcome to come to the cross

> I am a eunuch born this way from my mother's womb. I have a destiny in God.

of Jesus Christ. There is room there at the cross for all whom Christ died for, and it is my joy to meet people there day after day. I am thankful for this inclusive move of God's Spirit.

Today, I know who I am. I am a eunuch born this way from my mother's womb. I have a destiny in God. I have a high-calling that I am pursuing along with my life partner. Love fills my life. I have a wonderful family and a great Church. And to think that all of this was made possible because my life was turned upside down many years ago when I found myself in the eye of a storm—a storm about my sexuality.

One thing I have learned from my journey with God is that God is oftentimes in the storm. There are times in life when the waves of change seemingly are overwhelming yet that is exactly where God is. In fact, I have learned that when God is the source of the storm that is brewing, it is best to go with God. I am certain that you too have had the joy of riding out various storms in your life. We all need God's wisdom to help us identify whether the change that is sweeping through is from God or not from God.

As a Christian and a pastor based in California, I have recently been privy to a front row seat in a brewing storm. But this time the clouds that have been forming are concerning same-sex marriage. It all started when on May 15, 2008, the California Supreme Court ruled that it was unconstitutional to deny marriage to same-sex couples.[1] This ruling, you could say, opened up some powerful floodgates on all sides. It opened up the floodgates for same-sex couples to be legally married in California beginning on June 17, 2008. In a few short months there would be over 18,000 same-sex marriages conducted in California.[2] It also opened up the floodgates of opposition to same-sex marriage. The opposition to this historic California Supreme Court decision primarily came from segments of the religious community.

> One thing I have learned from my journey with God is that God is oftentimes in the storm.

The storm has continued to brew in California, as the debate over the constitutionality of same-sex marriages has first gone before the California Supreme Court, then to a Chief U.S. District Judge, and then more recently to the U.S. 9th District Appeals Court. On February 7, 2012, the federal appeals court struck down California's ban on same-sex marriage declaring that it violates the U.S. Constitution.[3] There is no doubt that this issue of same-sex marriage in the State of California, as well as in other states, will only continue to be discussed and resolved in future general elections and inevitably in cases that reach the Supreme Court of the land. However, this issue will also have to be resolved by the Church and that is why God's people are finding themselves on the forefront of this storm.

The question has been called in the State of California, regarding the right of same-sex couples to marry. At the heart of this controversy are age-old questions regarding the truth about homosexuality. "Is homosexuality a sin, a sickness, or a part of the spectrum of human sexuality?" "Is same-sex marriage sanctioned by God?" "Do gays and lesbians have gifts to offer the world?" "Should the Church welcome homosexuals if they follow Christ?" All of these questions are lurking behind the discussions wherever they are taking place.

From my vantage point as a Christian pastor and lesbian, I have a sense about who *really* has called the question regarding same-sex marriage. I believe Someone with a big agenda has put this issue front and center not only in California, but also in New York, Massachusetts, Connecticut, Iowa, Vermont, New Hampshire, Washington, Maine, Maryland, and in the District of Columbia. Since 2001, the legalization of same-sex marriage has swept through places like the Netherlands, Belgium, Canada, Spain, Iceland, South Africa, Norway, Sweden, Denmark, Portugal, Argentina, and Mexico. This does not even take into account the fifteen other nations that allow same-sex partnerships or unions such as the United Kingdom's Civil Partnership Act.

So, how did this happen? How did marriage get redefined in the *Merriam-Webster Dictionary* to include same-sex marriage?[4] A husband, wife, and 2.5 kids has been the traditional configuration for the notion of family in Western culture, but is this sacred "ideal" one that still exists today? Are these changes indicative of the decline of Christianity in America and other nations, or is it actually the reverse?

Could it be that heaven's got something to do with all of these changes? I believe heaven's floodgates have opened, and they are the most important and influential. I see a flurry of activity in the courtroom of heaven as God plays a hand in the affairs of a people group long denied justice and equality. It is as if the balcony of heaven has angelic hosts standing at attention, excitedly awaiting their assignments in the earth realm pertaining to this issue. Other angelic hosts take their place after returning from completing their assignments. All it takes is one word from the Almighty to cause a flurry of activity. What God has purposed from ages past is coming to fruition.

If there is a voice that needs to be heard at this time, it is God's voice. If there is a perspective we need for this season of change, it is God's perspective. We need to ask ourselves, "What is God saying?" A good place to start to discover where God stands on this issue is found in Psalm 9:7-9: "The Lord reigns forever; he has established his throne for judgment. He will judge the world in righteousness; he will govern the peoples with justice. The Lord is a refuge for the oppressed, a stronghold in times of trouble."

People don't often understand God's judgment. But God judges in order to bring justice to people who are oppressed. This is because God has always hated injustice and oppression. It is possible to be "religious" and still be on the wrong side of God's justice. We can be "religious" and be the ones that are actually oppressing others.

A foundational aspect of God is that God is Sovereign over all of the matters of our lives and the whole earth. God uses people to promote God's agenda at different times and in different generations. But, ultimately, God's truth is being unveiled throughout history. Yes, God is bringing the age old questions about homosexuality to the forefront. This book will attempt to discover what God's word has to say on this issue and then follow how God's truth is influencing the Church and society.

> It is possible to be "religious" and still be on the wrong side of God's justice. We can be "religious" and be the ones that are actually oppressing others.

Wherever you are at with the issue of homosexuality, I would like for us to begin by agreeing on one foundational truth about the Gospel. Is it not true that anyone who comes to Christ Jesus and believes in their heart and confesses with their mouth that Jesus rose from the dead and is Lord is a recipient of God's grace? After all, isn't God's love inclusive of all people and for the "whosoever? " I believe the Church in general would have a new perspective on homosexuality if it could comprehend the existence of gay and lesbian Christians. Many homosexuals are Bible believing Christians who love Jesus Christ and are saved by His blood. Recent research by the Barna Group confirms this, and indicates that one-third of gays and lesbians are Church-goers. Surprised? Also, the research shows that most gays and lesbians in America support Christianity, and one-sixth consider themselves to be born-again Christians.[5]

My heart's desire is to see Christians come together in unity regardless of differences. With this in mind, I went on an important prayer mission to Israel in the summer of 2006. I was also privileged to tour Israel which was a bit of an adventure since there was a war going on at the time. One of the most significant experiences I had was going with a group of other Christians to the house of Simon the Tanner in the city of Joppa. It was there on the rooftop of that house that Simon Peter, the Apostle to the Church, received the revelation from God that what God calls clean, is no longer unclean.[6] Peter was used by God to open the door of the Gospel to the Gentiles in a very dramatic way. It was so difficult for those early Jewish believers to fathom God's love for a people who were historically considered unclean and who were despised.

It was a memorable moment to stand there at that house and pray with my fellow Christians. We prayed that God would bring the same revelation that Peter received almost 2,000 years ago to other leaders in the Church worldwide today. We prayed for Church leaders in every nation to receive revelation from the Holy Spirit that gay and lesbian Christians are not unclean but are clean indeed! What is so interesting is that the father of our faith, Abraham, knew very well that he was called to be a blessing to the nations. Yet, the early Church who was immersed in the Spirit and covered in the merciful blood of Christ could not understand this fact. It seems that God has to chip away at prejudice in our lives because we so love to exclude those who are not like us.

The Church has historically been on the wrong side of acknowledging the glory of God in all of humanity. Was it not the early Church Fathers who erred in believing that women were somehow inferior to men and did not have souls? Perhaps we needed some early Church Mothers to help the Church see that both male and female are in the image of God. The Church also seemed to be the last to understand that women had more of a role in childbearing than simply incubating the seed of the male. It takes time for walls of ignorance and injustice to come down.

Later in history, it was the Church that upheld the lie that African-American slaves were on the bottom rung of human value. They were descendants of Ham, after all. The Bible speaks of slaves obeying their masters, so it was thought that a handful of Scriptures made the case for the nineteenth century's slave trade. Unfortunately, when something is a lie, even with a handful of Scriptures in your arsenal, you will find that it will not breed life, peace, or joy. Instead, the lie will be exposed, and eventually it won't function in society. That is what happened when people got close to their slaves and recognized the glory of God inherent within them. Yes, we've been wrong before. Let's not get it wrong with sexual minorities.

Fast-forward to today and tell me who the Church has historically considered unclean. You got it! Now, imagine that God is calling the question once and for all. The same God of the apostle Peter is breaking down mindsets, so that what God has spoken from the beginning of time will come to pass.

Is it possible that God has a perspective on the issue of homosexuality and is calling the question once and for all? I believe so. I trust that this book will be an avenue for God to bring truth and life into your heart regardless of where you stand on this issue.

God has called the question and a storm's a-brewing. But, listen up, and you just might hear God's voice speaking from out of the storm.

# 2

# THE GAY PROPAGANDA

**Pro pa gan da**
—Ideas, facts or allegations spread deliberately to further one's cause or to damage an opposing cause[7]
**A gen da**
—A list or outline of things to be considered or done
—An underlying often ideological plan or program[8]

In 1992, *The Report* produced a twenty-minute video called *The Gay Agenda*.[9] For many Christians, it provided a first look at the topic of homosexuality. After all, homosexuality has historically been considered an abomination by many Christians so much so that its name dared not be spoken. But when the "Gay '90s" arrived, suddenly everything gay became a hot topic. So, an evangelical Church in California created a video as a response.

*The Gay Agenda* video was supposed to be educational and, like its title indicated, it proposed that homosexuals had a certain agenda. In the end, its slanted views provided fodder within much of the Church for the growing fear and hatred of homosexuals. Why mention this video now? This video got widespread attention, and its fear-based message created a lasting impression upon many segments of the Church and society. This influential video eventually got into the hands of Pentagon officials in Washington, D.C.,[10] where President Clinton's efforts to lift a ban on homosexuals in the military failed miserably. This failure provided the scenario for the 1993 "Don't Ask, Don't Tell" policy which was not repealed until December 2010. Many in opposition to the President's intentions had been briefed by this video, so the outcome of this policy was no surprise.

When *The Gay Agenda* was first distributed in the early '90s, I heard rumors circulating about it. When I finally did view *The Gay Agenda*, I found out that it was anything but gay. In fact, I discovered that it was nothing more than propaganda. The definition of "propaganda" is the spreading of ideas, information, or rumor for the purpose of helping or injuring an institution, a cause, or a person.[11] The word was birthed when the Roman Catholic Church was given jurisdiction over missionary territories. What this means is that originally the word "propaganda" was for the purpose of spreading the Gospel message or "Good News." But, in the case of *The Gay Agenda*, this video was made to spread ideas for the purpose of injuring a cause or a person, namely, gays and lesbians.

Propaganda is always based in fear when its purpose is to injure. *The Gay Agenda* is in line with this type of propaganda because it was basically produced to warn heterosexuals everywhere that homosexuals are deviant.

> Propaganda is always based in fear when its purpose is to injure.

This video warned heterosexuals that gays and lesbians have an agenda to destroy society by targeting the very young. The type of fear that this video produced is called "homophobia"—which is an irrational fear of, or an aversion to, homosexuality or homosexuals.[12]

What I saw in *The Gay Agenda* was real video footage of a Gay Pride parade, the 1993 March on Washington, and gay activism in San Francisco. The majority of the dark and grainy video footage appeared to be from a Gay Pride parade, which eagerly provided the viewer with lasting images of topless women defiantly marching down the street, scantily dressed dancers on floats gyrating lewdly, and shots of children crying. To be sure, the raw footage was condemning of lurid behavior. But I question whether it is fair to condemn homosexuality based on some scenes from a Gay Pride parade. If so, then would it not be fair to condemn heterosexuality based on the same behavior exemplified by heterosexuals at say a Mardi Gras or in a TV show or movie with heterosexual characters?

This video also promoted supposed "expert" testimonials provided by two ex-gays, a doctor, a psychologist, and the president of the Western Center for Law & Religious Freedom. One of the ex-gay testimonials was given by John Paulk, introduced as the administrator of *Love in Action*, an ex-gay ministry. In one of the final segments of the video, a picture of John with his ex-lesbian wife Anne is shown while a voice-over states, "On July 19, 1992, John Paulk was married." This type of statement is like a trophy for ex-gay ministries. They believe that if someone actually marries heterosexually, then it is evidence that the homosexual individual has become heterosexual. How sad that this is not the case! If they could only feel the heartbreak of countless numbers of gays and lesbians who struggle daily to live in a heterosexual marriage. Many homosexuals do this because it is what they believe God, their pastors, or perhaps their families expect of them.

They say that hindsight is twenty-twenty vision and for this video, hindsight is devastating. You see, tragically, John Paulk is later defrocked from another ex-gay ministry sponsored by *Focus On The Family* called *Exodus International*. This demotion takes place after he is caught patronizing a gay bar and lying about it.[13]

While the story of John Paulk is heartbreaking, the expert testimonial by the supposed psychologist is misleading. Joseph Nicolosi, Ph. D. is introduced as the author of *Reparative Therapy of Male Homosexuality*. In his first segment as an expert he boasts that the gay movement is threatened by the kind of therapy he does. Nicolosi then goes on to explain that the gay movement is threatened because his therapy demonstrates that homosexuals can change. What is negligent about this kind of statement is how misleading it is. While reparative therapists, like most ex-gay organizations, claim that homosexuals can change, unfortunately, they do not clearly define what they mean by change. In fact, the change they are speaking about is not a transformation of one's sexuality. Rather, the change they offer focuses on behavioral changes that actually end up suppressing one's sexuality.

This is why the American Psychological Association passed a resolution in 1997 requiring informed consent from reparative therapists.[14] This means that those seeking reparative therapy as of 1997, have to be informed that major mental health associations oppose reparative therapy. Also, these therapists can no longer inform patients that homosexuality is unhealthy, a mental illness, or a lifestyle leading to unhappiness. It is truly poignant that the one and only psychologist featured in *The Gay Agenda* is a reparative therapist. Perhaps this is due to the fact that the American Psychiatric Association dropped homosexuality from its list of mental illnesses in 1973. America is not alone in this. The World Health Organization took the same stance in 1993, as did Japan's and China's psychiatric associations in 1995 and 2001.

Just recently, Exodus International, a leading force in the ex-gay movement worldwide, changed its position on homosexuality after thirty years of proposing a "cure" through prayer and psychotherapy.[15] In their July 2012 annual meeting, Alan Chambers, the president of Exodus International, shared how there was no "cure" for homosexuality and he even conceded that reparative therapy could be harmful. More poignantly, Chambers stated that every "ex-gay" he has ever met, including himself, still deals with homosexual cravings. I applaud Alan Chambers for his truthfulness, because it took a lot of courage for him to take this new stance on the position of being "ex-gay." Yet, my heart also breaks for Chambers since he continues to believe that homosexuality is sinful and opposed to the teachings of the Bible.

It is time for Christians to come together so that the Church can catch up to much of what society already embraces. It is not too late to let go of fear and even ignorance when it comes to homosexuality. It might be surprising to know that the only *agenda* that exists among sexual minorities is an attempt to enact changes within society that would extend equal rights to all people. Is that so wrong? Does this sound like something any member of society should fear?

Currently, Americans are debating how to approach the widespread plague of bullying in schools and specifically anti-gay bullying among teens.[16] Following an outbreak of gay teen suicides, schools are being forced to find solutions to the problem at hand. Since many schools already have anti-bullying programs, one solution that is being presented is to specifically address issues pertaining to harassment of gay youth in anti-bullying programs.

However, social conservatives view this type of education in the anti-bullying programs as simply a way for young people's minds to be swayed toward acceptance of homosexuality. In other words, they view speaking about gay, lesbian, bisexual, or transgender teens in schools and the harassment that is affecting them as nothing more than a pro-gay propaganda tool.

It is time for the Church to lead the way in solving the gay harassment problem instead of being fearful. In fact, several young men were influenced to commit suicide recently because of harassment, including Seth Walsh, thirteen, who tried to hang himself from a tree in his backyard; Justin Aaberg, fifteen, who hung himself in his room; Billy Lucas, fifteen, who hung himself from the rafters of a barn; and Tyler Clementi, eighteen, a Rutgers university freshman who jumped off the George Washington Bridge.

The teen suicide that really touched my heart was that of Asher Brown, thirteen, an eighth grader living in Houston, Texas. Asher shot himself after school one day with his stepfather's gun and was found by his stepfather in the closet where the gun was stored. Asher's parents stated that their son had been "bullied to death" by four students at the middle school he attended.[17] Apparently, Asher was harassed for his small size, his religion, for not wearing designer clothes and shoes, and he was also accused of being gay. In fact, some of the students even performed mock gay acts on him in his physical education class. The parents had complained about the bullying to the school officials for over eighteen months but felt that the complaints had only landed on deaf ears.

The morning of Asher's suicide, he had confided to his stepfather that he was gay. Thankfully, Asher's stepfather made known that he did not condemn Asher at all for being gay. Yet, young teens struggling with their homosexual orientation need much encouragement, affirmation, and support in order to overcome the harassment that they receive at the hands of family and peers. Wouldn't it be nice if the Church could provide support for young gay and lesbian teens that are just beginning to recognize their homosexual orientation in hostile environments?

In a response to the wave of gay teen suicides in America, a group of almost two dozen Houston area Churches designated Sunday, February 20, 2011, as "Bring Your Gay Teen to Church Day." These Churches wanted to focus on sharing a Christian message of love and acceptance to gay and lesbian teens as well as to their families. The Rev. Jim Bankston, senior minister at St. Paul's United Methodist Church in Houston, stated the reason why they had opted to be a part of the event, "We think it's important for families to know there's a safe place to go to worship. Families who have gay members want to make sure they feel welcome in Church and aren't bashed in any way."[18]

It is refreshing to know that positive change can occur in the world for those who find the world a hostile place. It is even more wonderful when the change occurs through the Church who is called to be the light of the world.

It is heartbreaking that over the last few years many Christian leaders have continued to voice their condemnation of gays and lesbians and have propagated the existence of some type of sinister

> It is heartbreaking that over the last few years many Christian leaders have continued to voice their condemnation of gays and lesbians and have propagated the existence of some type of sinister gay agenda.

*gay agenda.* When terrorists attacked the United States of America on September 11, 2001, Jerry Falwell, famed Southern Baptist pastor and speaker, blamed the attack on a variety of people which included gays and lesbians.[19] His voice was heard over the airwaves on the *700 Club,* with Pat Robertson agreeing, as they pointed the finger at homosexuals as partially to blame for the attack in New York City.

Famed pastor, author, and founder of World Challenge, David Wilkerson, penned a book in 1998, entitled *America's Last Call.* A large portion of his book is an outcry against homosexuality as one of the major reasons why God's judgment is coming to America. The tone of his book regarding homosexuality is obvious from the heading of the fifth chapter of his book entitled, "The Ominous Rise of Militant Homosexual Power."[20]

More recently, pastor and author, Francis Frangipane in his book *This Day We Fight,* encouraged Christians to engage in the spiritual battle surrounding them. One of the issues that Frangipane highlighted for the purposes of prayer was an aggressive "homosexual agenda."[21] While there is no doubt that these wonderful Christian leaders are well-meaning, it is also true that we can mean well but still error in the way that we understand, love, and speak about others.

And so the flames of fear continue to burn and be transmitted, oftentimes by well-meaning Christian people. Interestingly enough, David Kinnaman, the president of the Barna Group, recently co-wrote a book with Gabe Lyons entitled *Unchristian: What A New Generation Really Thinks About Christianity... And Why It Matters*, in which one of the major problems addressed is how Christians today have an anti-gay image. According to their research, the authors indicate that the anti-gay perception has reached critical mass because younger non-believers see Christianity as synonymous with irrational fear and hostility towards gays.[22]

Isn't it time for the love and compassion of Christ to win out in the Church? Since this counterfeit *gay agenda* was birthed in fear, I, for one believe it cannot withstand the rains of love that are pouring down from heaven. Isn't it true, after all that love never fails?[23] John, the Apostle wrote this about the power of love to conquer fear:

"God is love. Whoever lives in love lives in God, and God in Him. In this way, love is made complete among us so that we will have confidence on the day of judgment, because in this world we are like Him. There is no fear in love. But perfect love drives out fear, because fear has to do with punishment. The one who fears is not made perfect in love."[24]

As Christians, we need to reject fear and be relevant as we face up to the issues of our day. The 2007 movie *For the Bible Tells Me So* features a mother of a young suicide victim. The mother, Mary Lou Wallner, shared in the movie how her daughter, Anna, had come out to her while she was away at college. Yet, Mary Lou had refused to accept her daughter's homosexuality. This caused their mother-daughter relationship to be a deeply troubled one. Finally, on February 28, 1997, Mary Lou received word from her ex-husband that Anna had been found hanging from the bar in her closet. She had died alone. It was only then that Mary Lou began a deep soul-searching process in order to discover why she had not loved her daughter unconditionally.

Mary Lou Wallner also decided to re-examine what she had been taught all of her life by the Church about homosexuality. She began an intense study of biblical passages and also spoke to people about her questions. What Mary Lou discovered was that God's word does not condemn homosexuality. At this time Mary Lou and her husband travel full-time sharing the story of their daughter's death in hopes that they can educate others about the consequences of homophobia.[25]

> God's Gay Agenda is one that purposes for the world and the Church to know the uniqueness, calling, and gifts of His gay and lesbian children.

It is becoming more and more apparent to people everywhere that the *gay propaganda* message is not accurate. It doesn't seem to truthfully portray gay, lesbian, bisexual, or transgender people in a way that reflects who they are in their families, workplaces, or Churches. Christians of every affiliation are also discovering that the *gay propaganda* message does not have its origins in Scripture, although many well-meaning Christians would believe otherwise. There is new information and revelation available today about homosexuality which takes into account the context, culture, ancient religious cult practices, and original language of the Scriptures. As Christians we have a responsibility to newly inform ourselves about this important issue of sexuality and human diversity.

It is the purpose of this book to present to you the real *Gay Agenda*. This *Gay Agenda* was not birthed out of fear and it is not something that will bring destruction. The fact is, God has a *Gay Agenda* and is in the process of promoting it to the world. *God's Gay Agenda* goes beyond the establishment of justice and equality for all of His creation. *God's Gay Agenda* is one that purposes for the world and the Church to know the uniqueness, calling, and gifts of His gay and lesbian children. If the Church will not receive this agenda that comes from heaven, it will miss out on one of the greatest moves of God in the earth.

# 3

# Nothing New Under the Sun

"What has been will be again, what has been done will be done again; there is nothing new under the sun." ~Ecclesiastes 1:9

If God does have a *Gay Agenda* then there must be something, somewhere in God's word that speaks about God's purposes for homosexuals. God's word originates in heaven and is released in His time here on earth, bringing us truth.

As we look to God's word concerning the issue of homosexuality, it is important to begin with the topic of sexual orientation. Sexual orientation has been traditionally considered a modern concept and therefore not applicable to the ancient biblical text. In fact, the idea specifically of a homosexual orientation is viewed by many as non-existent in the Bible. I believe this is a mistaken belief.

It is my view that sexual orientations existed in individuals throughout history but were simply classified, lived out, or discussed in a variety of different ways. I concede that the development of categories indicating sexual preference is indeed a product of our modern Western thinking. It is in fact a modern concept to understand sexuality in terms of something that develops within an individual and then finds expression in their behavior. Yet, in my view, this does not negate the fact that sexual orientations still existed in the ancient world. To be sure, there are scholars who allow for the existence of sexual orientation in the ancient world, but under a variety of categories and with different terminology. We will take a look at how this is possible and then uncover the terminology that is rooted in the Bible which points to homosexual orientation.

Now, I know that many of you have seen the word *homosexual* in your Bible but the fact is, that word was coined by a Hungarian physician named Karoly Maria Benkert in 1869. The word *homosexual* gradually came to be the term used by scholars in the medical and social sciences to refer to people of same-sex orientation.[26] In fact, some form of the term *homosexual* in the biblical text is only a twentieth century inclusion. The term was never used by English Bible translators until 1946, when the Greek words *arsenokoitai* and *malakoi* were translated into English as *homosexuals*.[27] The problem with these two Greek words is that they are translated in different ways even within English Bible translations, simply because their meanings are layered.

What we want to discover is if the Bible contains a term for homosexuality that originated in the biblical text itself and is confirmed by extra-biblical sources. Is this possible even though the idea of sexual orientation as we know it today was not fully developed during the time when the biblical writers were penning the Scriptures? I believe it is not only possible, but that such a word does exist. You see, although it is true that sexual orientation was not discussed in categories commonly known today, there is no doubt that there has been in existence terminology associated with people who had same-sex attractions, same-sex sexual practices, or were known to have same-sex partners. There are also historical records of how people responded to those with known same-sex attractions.

An example of this is found in the saying, *cut sleeve*, a popular Chinese euphemism for homosexuals. It seems that in 6 BC, the Chinese Emperor Ai-Ti was sleeping in his bed with his young lover Tung who was lying on the Emperor's sleeve. In order to get up so he could attend to his imperial duties, it is said that the Emperor cut his sleeve off so as not to disturb his lover. Even to this day, the term *cut sleeve* is synonymous with *homosexual*.[28]

Another example of this is found when King James I succeeded Elizabeth to the English throne in 1603. Apparently, many poked fun at him behind his back by saying, "Elizabeth was King, now James is Queen."[29] It is no wonder that the Bible written under his charge is jokingly referred to as the *Queen James Bible!*

As far as terminology associated with same-sex sexual practices, we don't need to look any further than the Scriptures. In the Old Testament, the Hebrew word for priest is a good place for us to start. There is a distinction in the Hebrew text between the priests of Yahweh called *qadash*[30] and the priests dedicated to pagan deities called *qadesh*.[31] The first Hebrew word means "to be holy" while *qadesh* refers to "a sacred person, a male devotee (by prostitution) to licentious idolatry, and unclean."[32]

What many Christians fail to realize when they are reading their Bibles is that cultic religions were an institutionalized part of the ancient eastern world of the Bible. God hated the pagan worship practices of the nations, which is why the Bible clearly differentiates between God's priests and those that served pagan deities. Unfortunately, the Hebrew nation didn't hate these cultic religious practices as much. It wasn't long before these practices gained popularity among the Hebrew people and were eventually practiced, of all places, in Solomon's temple. Two kings of Judah, Asa

What many Christians fail to realize when they are reading their Bibles is that cultic religions were an institutionalized part of the ancient eastern world of the Bible.

and Josiah, were both commended for removing the idolatrous priests from Jerusalem during their reigns.[33] Josiah even removed the idolatrous priests from the temple!

A prohibition found in Deuteronomy 23:18-19 lends insight into the male-to-male sex practices of these pagan priests.

> "There shall be no ritual harlot [qedeshah, #6948] of the daughters of Israel, or a perverted one [qadesh, #6945] of the sons of Israel. You shall not bring the wages of a harlot [zanah, #2181] or the price of a dog [keleb, #3611] to the house of the Lord your God for any vowed offering, for both of these are an abomination to the Lord your God."[34] *(New King James Version)*

The first two types of people referred to by the terms *qedeshah* and *qadesh* are pagan priestesses and priests. The term *qedeshah,* meaning pagan priestesses and *zonah,* referring to female prostitutes, were at times used interchangeably. What I would like to draw your attention to here is the term *qadesh* for the male priest, because it is linked with male-to-male cultic activity. Notice that the counterpart to *qadesh* in the parallel construction of the two verses is *keleb,* or the term *dog*, in English. This is a derogatory term for someone who has intercourse in a dog-like position. This particular term, *keleb,* is identified on a Phoenician inscription on Cyprus dating back to the fourth century BC, showing a worker in the temple of Astarte.[35] Also, it is interesting that the Sumerogram for a male cult prostitute called *assinu* depicts the symbols for *dog* and *woman* joined together.[36]

These insights into male cultic activities are helpful when we relate them to God's prohibitions to the Hebrew people of "not lying with a man as one lies with a woman" found in Leviticus 18:22 and 20:13. The biblical message against cultic sexual activity is even reiterated at the end of the New Testament when Revelation 22:15 excludes dogs from the new Jerusalem, the Holy City. The terms for male pagan priest and prostitute allow us to see that the biblical text does contain terminology associated with same-sex sexual practices, although, so far all we have seen are terms related only to male-to-male cultic religious practices.

It is erroneous to think that there was a void in known same-sex activities during the time of Jesus' earthly ministry or during the time when the New Testament was being written. Nero, who became the Roman Emperor in 54 AD, was a contemporary of the apostle Paul. Emperor Nero was known to have married two men, one right after the other in public ceremonies. The Greeks and the Romans recognized the union with Spores, a castrated young man, and he was honored as Empress.[37] Nero was also known to have a famous lover named Narcissus. In Romans 16:11, the apostle Paul writes a greeting to the household of Narcissus. Many early Church historians like Dio Cassius (AD 155–AD 229) thought that it was actually Narcissus who interceded with Nero on behalf of the apostle Paul resulting in Paul's acquittal after his first arrest.[38]

The concept of sexual orientation might be a modern perspective on sexuality but sexual preferences nevertheless existed in individuals in ancient cultures. God created humanity perfectly as His crowning achievement, and part of that creation includes the aspect of sexuality. What we will find is that there is nothing new under the sun. In fact, there was language used in various cultures to refer to what is today called homoeroticism or same-sex orientation.

In his book *Homoeroticism in the Biblical World,* Old Testament scholar Martti Nissinen discusses how sexual encounters between people of the same sex were defined more in terms of gender. Yet, Nissinen does allow that sexual orientations existed in ancient cultures. In speaking of heterosexuality, bisexuality, and homosexuality, he states:

> These categories of sexual orientation represent a modern classification and cannot be found in ancient sources. The demarcation of homosexuality and heterosexuality presupposes a conceptualization of 'sexuality.' It corresponds with modern Western thinking, but may be less useful in the study of ancient cultures. This does not mean that various individual sexual orientations

would not have existed among ancient people. Persons with such preferences do appear in ancient sources, and their existence was noted and commented on by their contemporaries.[39]

Further support for the fact that sexual orientation would have been noted in various ways for ancient people is discussed by Bernadette Brooten in her work entitled, *Love Between Women*. In her work, centered upon early Christian responses to female homoeroticism, she writes that an understanding of erotic orientation would have been available to both Christian and non-Christian writers.

> Although ancient Christian writers resembled their non-Christian contemporaries in their views on erotic love between women, both groups differed from our own culture in their overall understanding of erotic orientation. Whereas we often dualistically define sexual orientation as either homosexual or heterosexual, they saw a plethora of orientations. (When we in the late twentieth century think about it, we also recognize bisexuals and transsexuals, leading us to speak of a spectrum, rather than a bifurcation.) Their matrix of erotic orientations included whether a person took an active or a passive sexual role, as well as the gender, age, nationality, and economic, legal (slave or free), and social status of the partner.[40]

What these sources indicate is that ancient people did recognize what we know today to be same-sex orientation, although modern terminology and perhaps categories of sexuality were not used. Much of how the ancient cultures viewed sexual expression had to do with the concept of gender and then in terms of active and passive sexual roles. The passive role in relationship was normally assigned to females, so if males were categorized as passive, they were considered feminine or out of the norm of masculinity. If a female was discovered to be the active partner in a sexual role, then she was labeled masculine. In these cultures, masculinity was considered superior and relationships were defined by the role or status of the male.

Also, the predominant familial structure modeled in the ancient world was a heterosexual marriage model that produced children. Sexual relationships did exist, however, outside of the heterosexual marriage model. For example, in many ancient cultures it was neither uncommon nor frowned upon for husbands to have sexual liaisons outside of the marriage unit. These liaisons could take place with female or male, free or slave, and with young or older partners. This is all the more reason to not negate same-sex orientation in persons simply because they happen to also be in a marriage union.

In many parts of the ancient East, it was also common for soldiers to have sexual relationships with other males. The male partners involved in these sexual relationships with soldiers could fall into the category of either free men or slaves. A biblical example of this type of relationship is found in the biblical account of the centurion soldier and his sick servant provided for us in the Gospels of Matthew and Luke.[41] Between the two biblical accounts two Greek words for "servant" are used—*pais* and *doulos*. Culturally, the Greek word *pais* could variously be interpreted to mean a son, a house servant, or even a male lover.[42] However, the Greek word *doulos* was never used for a son, leaving us with only two possibilities for the servant's true identity—a general servant or a lover. It is interesting that Matthew has the centurion using the term *pais* whenever he is speaking about his sick servant and then *doulos* for servants in general. This indicates that Matthew used the term *pais* to indicate that the sick servant is indeed a male lover in contrast to the other general servants who are called *doulos*. This is only confirmed by

> The fact that the word eunuch has any relationship to same-sex orientation has been but almost completely lost to biblical scholars and commentators over the years because there has not been much interest or research done in the study of eunuchs.

Luke who only uses the word *doulos* in his account but who describes the servant in Luke 7:2 as an *entimos doulos* meaning "dear, precious, or valuable"[43] servant. This leads us to believe that indeed the centurion sought Jesus to heal his dear or precious lover.

The fact is there were various terms applied to people in these ancient cultures who were known for what we today call same-sex orientation, or the preference of the same-sex over the opposite sex. One such term is deeply embedded in the biblical text. It is the word *eunuch*. The fact that the word *eunuch* has any relationship to same-sex orientation has been but almost completely lost to biblical scholars and commentators over the years because there has not been much interest or research done in the study of eunuchs. Also, words tend to have a way of evolving over time, and bias or tradition can have a way of putting blinders on us. Yet, it is the word *eunuch* that holds special meaning for us in the search for terminology that refers to homosexual orientation.

It is Jesus himself who teaches on the subject of *eunuchs* according to the Gospel of Matthew.[44] Jesus speaks about eunuchs in terms of those born as eunuchs, then those who are made eunuchs, and finally, those who make themselves eunuchs for the kingdom of heaven's sake. When Jesus' message on eunuchs is applied as the backdrop for our understanding of eunuchs, then it is striking how other scriptural references and also extra-biblical ancient writings only confirm his message.

# 4

# RED LETTER EUNUCHS

"Whatever exists has already been named, and what man is has
been known; no man can contend with one who is stronger than he."
~Ecclesiastes 6:10

Jesus was not just a good man; he was and is the Son of God.
Therefore, when he spoke, his words carried authority. All of
heaven endorsed his words. Jesus' words are highlighted in red in many
Bibles. This chapter is dedicated to understanding *red letter eunuchs*.
Jesus' words in Matthew 19:12 should be our standard when speaking
about eunuchs. The fact is Jesus spoke about a people who were not
always spoken about so favorably. His comments about eunuchs broke
through negative stereotypes at the time and bring clarity for us today.

Although Jesus spoke with real authority, His teachings both amazed
people and angered them. The religious rejected his teachings. Yet, for

the people who were open to hear, they were amazed at the authority and wisdom that flowed from his lips. I can imagine the scenario of Matthew 19:1-12. There is Jesus, cornered by the Pharisees, with his disciples watching to see what Jesus would do and say. When asked about divorce, Jesus set the record straight on both marriage and divorce. Then, Jesus taught on the subject of eunuchs.

It is at the end of his teaching in Matthew 19:11 and 12 that Jesus says some pretty amazing things about eunuchs.

> "But he said unto them, 'All cannot accept this saying, but only those to whom it has been given: For there are eunuchs who were born thus from their mother's womb, and there are eunuchs who were made eunuchs by men, and there are eunuchs who have made themselves eunuchs for the kingdom of heaven's sake. He who is able to accept it, let him accept it." (NKJV)

I see the scenario of Matthew 19:1-12 as a heated debate between Jesus and some religious leaders. What is significant is that at the end of this debate, Jesus brings up a taboo subject. Of all people, he brings up eunuchs! Jesus stands there in front of these religious leaders and speaks to them of a people who were in some cases often despised and historically not even allowed in the temple. With his words, Jesus sought to not only confront the religious beliefs of the religious leaders of his day, but his words also echo down through the ages to prepare a modern eunuch people for their destiny. That is why Jesus concluded his remarks by saying, "He who is able to accept it, let him accept it."[45]

Jesus must have known that his words would be accepted one day and that they would be especially powerful in the ears of future generations.

The importance of this cannot be underestimated. Either the Greek word *eunouchos* or the Aramaic word *saris* came from Jesus' lips—not just once but several times. It is time that we understand *red letter eunuchs* and grasp exactly what Jesus meant when he taught his disciples and the religious leaders of his day about them.

It has been defended for quite some time that Jesus said nothing about homosexuality. Jesus' supposed silence on the subject has been used by some as affirmation that he was not condemning of people with a same-sex orientation. In spite of this, I believe that Jesus did speak about homosexuality when he spoke about born eunuchs. Furthermore, I see that in the account of the centurion and his servant lover and in other instances which we will touch on, Jesus' words and his actions were affirming of homosexuals.[46]

> It has been defended for quite some time that Jesus said nothing about homosexuality.

*Eunuch* is the word that Jesus chose in order to provide affirmation for modern homosexuals.[47] As we go through this study on the word *eunuch*, I believe that you will begin to see that perhaps our modern understanding of eunuchs has been flawed. It is important for us to re-evaluate what we know about eunuchs based on what God's word says about them.

To begin with, Jesus first mentioned that there were "eunuchs born thus from their mother's womb." What Jesus was addressing here would have been known by his contemporaries as *natural eunuchs*, or *born eunuchs*. We will name the eunuchs in Jesus' first category as *natural-born eunuchs*. This first category of eunuchs parallels what we understand today to be gays and lesbians.

Then, Jesus went on to speak about "eunuchs who were made eunuchs by men" or what were known as *man-made eunuchs*. It is no doubt that this second category is referring to castrated males. What we will see is that both *natural-born eunuchs* and *man-made eunuchs* were well-known categories of eunuchs that were widely used in the ancient East for approximately 800 to 1,000 years. Jesus' contemporaries would have known about these two categories of eunuchs, which is why it is important for us to understand them, too. In mentioning both *natural-born eunuchs* and *man-made eunuchs,* Jesus sought to clearly reveal not only their existence, but also their distinction.

Now that we have briefly identified Jesus' first two categories of eunuchs, let's take a good look at the word *eunuch* as it is used in the

Bible. The English word *eunuch* which comes from the Greek word *eunouchos* is found in the New Testament in only two places. First, it is found twice in the words of Jesus in Matthew 19:12 and then five times in the story of the Ethiopian eunuch finding salvation in Acts 8:27-39.[48] The Greek word *eunouchos* is made up of two words: *eun,* for bed, and *echein,* to keep. Also, in Matthew 19:12 Jesus used twice the related Greek word—*eunouchizo,* which simply means to make a eunuch.[49] The Greek word *eunouchos,* according to the *Strong's Exhaustive Concordance of the Bible,* refers to "a castrated person (being employed in Oriental bed chambers) by extension an impotent or unmarried man, by implication a chamberlain (state officer)."[50]

As far as the Old Testament is concerned, the Hebrew counterpart for *eunuch* is *saris,* which is used forty-two times in the Hebrew text.[51] A related word, *Rabsaris,* originally an Assyrian word, is used three times. The *Strong's Exhaustive Concordance of the Bible* offers the meaning for *saris* as: "to castrate, a eunuch, a valet, and especially of female apartments, and a minister of the state."[52] The word *Rabsaris* is really the equivalent of *saris* and is used in all three instances as a title referring to one of Nebuchadnezzer's high ranking officials and to an officer of Sennacherib, the Assyrian king.[53] The term *Rab* simply means *abundant* but specifically with *saris,* it has the meaning of chief eunuch, a high official, or head of the eunuchs.[54]

It is fascinating that recently the Rabsaris or chief eunuch of King Nebuchadnezzar II made headlines. In 2007, the name of the Rabsaris of King Nebuchadnezzar II was identified on a 2,500-year-old stone tablet by the Austrian Assyriologist, Michael Jursa.[55] Although the stone was discovered earlier in 1920 and held at the British Museum, the tablet written in Babylonian cuneiform was only recently translated by Jursa when the cuneiform code was finally cracked. The tablet confirmed Jeremiah's account of the siege of Jerusalem as indicated in Jeremiah 39:3. The tablet is a historical record that tells us Nebo-Sarsekim, chief eunuch to Nebuchadnezzar II, paid gold to the temple of Babylon. The discovery of the ancient tablet and its subsequent translation serve to remind us of the important status of many eunuchs in the ancient world.

It is possible that since Jesus spoke Aramaic he would have originally spoken the Hebrew and Aramaic word *saris* instead of the Greek word *eunouchos* of Matthew 19:12. Whichever the case, it is clear that the word *eunuch* is safely embedded in the biblical texts stemming from either the Greek word *eunouchos* or its Hebrew counterpart, *saris*.

So, who are *red-letter eunuchs* and what did Jesus have in mind when he talked about them to his disciples and the religious leaders of his day? In order to understand the context of Jesus' words about eunuchs, let's take a look at some extra biblical writings that highlight both of these categories for us. There is extra-biblical information on the category of *natural-born eunuchs* and quite a bit of historical information on *man-made eunuchs* because the practice of castration was so prevalent in many ancient civilizations. What distinguished the *natural-born eunuchs* from the *man-made eunuchs,* besides the issue of castration, was the fact that *natural-born eunuchs* were known for their disinterest in marriage, their disinterest in sexual relations with women, and for their same-sex attraction.

> Jesus lived under Roman law. Here we see how Roman law confirms that there were known categories of eunuchs.

To begin with, Roman law seems to corroborate Jesus' categories of eunuchs.[56] *The Digest of Justinian* is a compilation of over 1,000 years of Roman law as commissioned by Emperor Justinian. It centers on the writings of Roman legal experts of which Ulpian seems to be one of the foremost experts on Roman law. It is Ulpian (172-223 AD) who writes the following regarding eunuchs:

> "The name of eunuch is a general one; under it come those who are eunuchs by nature, those who are made eunuchs, and any other kind of eunuchs."[57]

Jesus lived under Roman law. Here we see how Roman law confirms that there were known categories of eunuchs. It seems that it was common to refer to eunuchs as both "eunuchs by nature" and then "made eunuchs." This reference indicates that it was understood by the Romans that there were those who were natural-born eunuchs as opposed to man-made eunuchs. It also suggests that there were other types of eunuchs.

The fact that there were eunuchs who were not castrated is clear from the Roman law. In fact, the Roman law touched on whether a eunuch could marry or not. Ulpian goes on to provide instructions on marriages with eunuchs in the following:

> "Where a woman marries a eunuch, I think that a distinction must be drawn between a man who has been castrated and one who has not, so that if he has been castrated, you may say that there cannot be a dowry; but where a man has not been castrated, there can be a dowry and an action for it, because a marriage can take place here."[58]

This reference seems to suggest that a marriage between a woman and a castrated eunuch was not to be undertaken. Why eunuchs, both natural-born or man-made would want to marry is not clear from this text. However, what is clear here is that again there was a distinction in the mind of the Roman people between a eunuch who was one by nature and one who was made a eunuch through castration.

*Natural-born eunuchs* were also identified by the Jews although the Hebrew term *saris* is used. A humorous—though not flattering—description of *natural-born eunuchs* is provided by various Jewish rabbis in the Babylonian Talmud called the *Yebamoth* in the following:

> R. Joseph said: It must have been such a saris [6] of whom I heard Ammi saying. 'He who is afflicted from birth', [7] … Our Rabbis taught: Who is a congenital saris? [13] Any person who is twenty years of age and has not produced two pubic hairs. [14] And even if he produced them afterwards he is deemed to be a saris in all respects. And these are his characteristics: He has no beard. His hair

is lank, and his skin is smooth. R. Simeon b. Gamaliel said in the name of R. Judah b. Jair: [15] Any person whose urine produces no froth; some say: He who urinates without forming an arch; some say: He whose semen is watery; and some say: He whose urine does not ferment. Others say: He whose body does not steam after bathing in the winter season. R. Simeon b. Eleazar said: [15] He whose voice is abnormal so that one cannot distinguish whether it is that of a man or a woman.[59]

The Babylonian Talmud indicates that there was an understanding among Jewish rabbis about males who were known to be eunuchs from birth. They identify what Jesus termed to be "eunuchs born thus from their mother's womb" as "He who is afflicted from birth," or a "congenital saris." There is agreement therefore between Jesus and these Jewish rabbis on eunuchs who were natural-born eunuchs. Natural-born eunuchs apparently could not choose to become eunuchs since it was common knowledge that these eunuchs were born as such.

It is interesting that the rabbis do not speak favorably of these eunuchs and, in fact, consider them to be "afflicted." Yet, the words of Jesus in Matthew 19:12 are in no way condemning of eunuchs. Rather, what we will see when we discuss Jesus' third category of eunuchs is that Jesus not only speaks favorably about eunuchs but He also elevates their status as those who are set apart for the kingdom of heaven.

An interesting observation about this reference to eunuchs in Judaism is that there seems to be an understanding that these eunuchs who are "afflicted from birth" are able to produce semen. This leads us to believe that it was understood historically by Jewish leaders that *natural-born eunuchs* were not castrated nor were they genitally deformed.

What is also critical to note, is that in the Jewish culture, the ability or willingness to procreate is of utmost importance. If natural-born eunuchs are not interested in women sexually, then that would most likely explain the unfavorable disposition of the rabbis towards them. In fact, the rabbis describe these eunuchs in terms of being cold or lacking in passion. For example, their semen is described as watery and their bodies as not steaming after a bath. These descriptions which were usually associated with women make sense when Aristotle's influence is understood on the subject.

According to Aristotle, women's bodies were too cold to give form to semen (*Generation of Animals* 2.7). In fact, women could not produce children without men because their fluids were not generative. Aristotle reasoned that it was the heat of passion in a male's climax that caused the semen to become generative, and therefore, procreation possible. So, in context, the rabbis seem to be indicating that these eunuchs who are afflicted are in fact unable to feel the heat of passion like other hot-blooded males. I would venture to say that these natural eunuchs appear to be lacking in passion because they are simply disinterested in women.

In case you were thinking that all of the references to eunuchs were going to be references solely to male eunuchs, think again. The Babylonian Talmud, Tractate Yebamoth 80a continues on with this description of a female saris:

> What woman is deemed to be incapable of procreation? Any woman who is twenty years of age and has not produced two pubic hairs. [14] And even if she produces them afterwards she is deemed to be a woman incapable of procreation in all respects. And these are her characteristics: She has no breasts and suffers pain during copulation... R. Simeon b. Eleazar said: One whose voice is deep so that one cannot distinguish whether it is that of a man or of a woman.[60]

What we see here is that the female eunuch is spoken about in terms of being incapable of procreating. She is described as suffering pain during copulation. One can only imagine how this fact is discovered. What this seems to highlight is the fact that the female eunuchs were not appreciative of this type of sexual liaison. And once again, it is likely that the disinterest on the part of the male and female natural-born eunuchs is because they are not interested sexually in the opposite sex.

There are other references to female eunuchs, both natural-born and man-made, in extra-biblical texts. This is why we can relate Jesus' first category of *natural-born eunuch* to mean male and female homosexuals.

So far, we have already been introduced to the female *saris* from the Babylonian Talmud. Although the feminine term *sarisa* is not used in the biblical text, it is found in the Talmud to refer to female eunuchs.[61] According to Bernadette Brooten, author of *Love Between Women*, ancient Judaism did not seem to be strictly opposed to sexual love between women, but simply emphasized the importance of women being prepared for marriage to future husbands. Indeed, it was a necessity for women to marry and exist within the framework of heterosexual marriage.[62] Brooten also discusses in her book counterpart terms for the female eunuch as *tribas* for the Greeks and *virago* in Latin.[63] All in all, there is a need for much more research to be done in the area of female eunuchs since the Bible is not explicit on the subject and the known extra-biblical information is limited.

> Not only did the Romans and the Jews have knowledge of eunuchs as we have seen, but Christians too were familiar with both natural-born eunuchs and man-made eunuchs.

Not only did the Romans and the Jews have knowledge of eunuchs as we have seen, but Christians too were familiar with both *natural-born eunuchs* and *man-made eunuchs*. There are a couple of interesting references to eunuchs included in the Apocrypha.[64] The Wisdom of Solomon 3:14, which was written in the first or second century BC, mentions eunuchs who engage in masturbation. This book is one of the deuterocanonical books in that it is not a part of the Jewish Bible but is included in the Apocrypha. A second reference in the Apocrypha to eunuchs is found in Wisdom of Sirach 30:20. Here, mention is made to a eunuch embracing a woman while eliciting a groan. The implication is that the eunuch had no interest in a woman.

Also, one of the early Church fathers, Clement of Alexandria (150-215AD) wrote about eunuch servants, warning Christians of their evils. Clement of Alexandria warned those in Christian households against entrusting wives to eunuch servants. He stated this about eunuchs:

> "Many are eunuchs; and these panders, serve without suspicion those that wish to be free to enjoy their

pleasures, because of the belief that they are unable to indulge in lust. But a true eunuch is not one who is unable, but one who is unwilling, to indulge in pleasure."[65]

Although the comments of Clement of Alexandria appear on the outset to not be very favorable toward eunuchs in general, they actually reveal an understanding of the distinction between *man-made eunuchs* and *natural-born eunuchs* and edify natural-born eunuchs as "true eunuchs."

First, Clement of Alexandria warns Christian men against having eunuchs manage their households because they are a threat to their wives. The reason for this threat is because *man-made eunuchs* were oftentimes able to indulge in lust or sexual misconduct, especially if castrated post puberty. Clement was saying that Christian men and women were to be aware of these types of *man-made eunuchs*. On the other hand, Clement of Alexandria goes on to identify *natural-born eunuchs* to be "true eunuchs." He indicates that these true eunuchs, though able to have sexual relations with women, are simply unwilling to do so. In other words, Clement of Alexandria recognizes true eunuchs to be unwilling sexual partners for women because they were not attracted to them. It seems that there is a parallel between Clement of Alexandria's true eunuchs and modern-day eunuchs or homosexuals.

An even more conclusive writing by Clement of Alexandria on how natural-born eunuchs are disinterested in sexual relations with women is found in his discussion about the Basilidian Christians who were gnostics. Clement of Alexandria reveals the thinking of his contemporaries when he writes this about eunuchs:

> The Valentinians, who hold that the union of man and woman is derived from the divine emanation in heaven above, approve of marriage. The followers of Basilides, on the other hand, say that when the apostles asked whether it was not better not to marry, the Lord replied: "Not all can receive this saying; there are some eunuchs who are so from their birth, others are so of necessity." And their explanation of this saying is roughly as follows: Some men, from their birth, have a natural sense of

repulsion from a woman; and those who are naturally so constituted do well not to marry.[66]

In addressing how the Basilidian Christians understood Jesus' words in Matthew 19:12, we see that Clement of Alexandria once again mentioned two different types of eunuchs. He mentions "eunuchs from birth" and "eunuchs of necessity." He then goes on to state that the Basilidian Christians implicitly understood the eunuchs from birth to have a repulsion for women. These Gnostic Christians saw this repulsion as a natural thing for these natural-born eunuchs. Finally, these Gnostic Christians encouraged these natural-born eunuchs to not marry.

During the Council of Nicea, an important landmark for Christian formation which took place in 325 AD, the topic of ministry among eunuchs was addressed. Attending the council were 300 bishops who made a decision regarding eunuchs in ministry. They determined that *natural-born eunuchs* along with certain *man-made eunuchs* could participate in ministry and, specifically, in the role of bishop as long as they were found worthy of the honor. One of the decrees from this landmark meeting is as follows:

> "A eunuch, if he has been made so by the violence of men or if his virilia have been amputated in times of persecution, or if he has been born so, if in other respects he is worthy, may be made a bishop."[67]

What we see here is that the bishops of the Church in the fourth century decided that *natural-born eunuchs* could be full participants in the Church. Not only that, but *natural-born eunuchs* could also serve as bishops. In addition, the Council's decree also stipulated that *man-made eunuchs* who specifically did not choose to be castrated could be full participants and serve in the Church as bishops. The key to the inclusion of man-made eunuchs in the Church was involuntary castration.

Another Church father, Gregory of Nazianzus (329-389 AD), around this same time addressed the topic of eunuchs in the Church. He writes specifically about *natural-born eunuchs* and what is natural for them as follows:

For there are eunuchs which were made eunuchs from their mother's womb. I should very much like to be able to say something bold about eunuchs. Be not proud, ye who are eunuchs by nature. For, in point of self-restraint, this is perhaps unwilling. For it has not come to the test, nor has your self-restraint been proved by trial. For the good which is by nature is not a subject of merit; that which is the result of purpose is laudable. What merit has fire for burning, for it is its nature to burn? What merit has water for falling, a property given to it by its Maker? What thanks does the snow get for its coldness, or the sun for its shining? It shines even if it does not wish… Since then, natural chastity is not meritorious, I demand something else from the eunuchs. Do not go a whoring in respect of the Godhead. Having been wedded to Christ, do not dishonor Christ.[68]

This reference by Gregory of Nazianzus is remarkable because he is clearly addressing natural-born eunuchs who are in his congregation. He uses the very words of Jesus and states that they are "eunuchs which were made eunuchs from their mother's womb." Here Gregory of Nazianzus is speaking of Christian eunuchs who are described as "wedded to Christ." He also states that these natural-born eunuchs, by no matter of their will, are disinterested in women. It is natural for these eunuchs to have self-restraint with women although perhaps unwilling. Their natural inclination to not be interested in the opposite sex is seen by Gregory of Nazianzus as not really praiseworthy because it is natural like the sun shining. These words of this Christian leader help us to understand how the Church during this period dealt with natural-born eunuchs.

Although Gregory of Nazianzus has described these natural-born eunuchs as having "natural chastity" presumably in regards to women, he goes on to speak about their sexual conduct. He encourages these natural-born eunuchs in his congregation to live lives worthy of their Christian calling. As Christians, they are instructed to honor Christ by not engaging in sexual relations deemed to be "whoring" by Gregory. You might wonder what type of "whoring" is connected to the

"Godhead." I believe this warning by this Christian leader is for those natural-born eunuchs who would feel drawn to idolatrous practices. In fact, one of the earliest known roles for man-made eunuchs was in cultic religious practices. Pagan priests and temple prostitutes were involved not only in physical fornication, so to speak, but were also engaged in spiritual fornication by going after these false gods. These cultic religious practices might have been a source of temptation for Christian eunuchs if indeed they were homosexual men, as we are suggesting. The temptation would only exist if these Christian eunuchs were attracted to other men and drawn to places where same-sex cultic practices were prevalent.

Later in his writings, Gregory of Nazianzus does clearly mention cultic prostitution when he states "For it is not only bodily sin which is called fornication and adultery, but any sin you have committed, and especially transgression against that which is divine. Perhaps you ask how we can prove this: 'They went a whoring, it says, with their own inventions.'"[69] What is quoted here by Gregory of Nazianzus is Psalm 107:39, which is a reference to the Hebrew nation's pursuit and involvement in Canaan's cultic religious practices. This verse states: "They defiled themselves by what they did; by their deeds they prostituted themselves."[70] So, again, what Gregory of Nazianzus is warning the natural-born eunuchs in his congregation against is sexual activity with other males in a cultic environment. This, I believe, is further proof that Gregory of Nazianzus, like other Christian leaders before him, understood that natural-born eunuchs were attracted naturally to other men.

> What is also wonderful is that Christian natural-born eunuchs were welcomed as full participants in the early Church.

So far, we have seen that there is extra-biblical support for the words of Jesus in Matthew 19:12 regarding *natural-born eunuchs*. Descriptions of these natural-born eunuchs parallel what we would deem to be persons of homosexual orientation. The natural-born eunuchs are described as eunuchs from birth. In other words, these natural-born eunuchs did not choose to become eunuchs but were eunuchs from their mother's womb. These natural-born eunuchs are described in extra-biblical writings as not interested in the opposite sex. They also are described as attracted to people of the same sex. What is also wonderful is that Christian natural-born eunuchs were welcomed as full participants in the early Church. Furthermore, the Council of Nicea stipulated that eunuchs could become leaders in the Church, even bishops. Any general disdain about eunuchs seems to be centered on castration, and as we saw with the bishops in the Council of Nicea, where castration was accepted voluntarily. This is all good news for modern-day eunuchs or gays and lesbians.

This brings us to Jesus' second category of eunuchs. If natural-born eunuchs are examples of people of homosexual orientation, then what are man-made eunuchs? Jesus obviously had something in mind when he spoke about this second category of eunuch. In fact, Jesus was informed by his environment and the first century culture of the East.

There is a vast array of extra-biblical material on what Jesus described as "eunuchs who have been made eunuchs by men." Jesus lived during a time when the Roman Empire ruled Israel giving him knowledge of "man-made eunuchs." A few years after Jesus' death, in the first century AD, the Roman Emperor Domitian tried to outlaw the practice of castration with little success. The practice was difficult to stop due to the trade demands for castrated boys. This practice endured even into the early nineteenth century with the use of castrated boys who sang soprano in the Sistine Chapel.[71]

The practice of castration evidently existed for many years in ancient civilizations among the Egyptians, Persians, Assyrians, Ethiopians, Medes, and even the Chinese.[72] It seems that the first written record of eunuchs comes from China around the twelfth century before Christ. It is thought that China has had the longest uninterrupted history of castrated eunuchs going back 5,000 years, but many of their records were destroyed by the Emperor Ch'in shih huang Ti (246-201 BC) when he ordered books on history, astronomy, and classical literature to be burned. Regardless, a hint about the Chinese practices with eunuchs is seen in that the central character of the most common Chinese word for eunuch means both *palace* and *castration*.[73]

The Persian use of eunuchs is recorded as carvings on the walls of Nineveh and also on the walls of Assyrian palaces dating 1000 BC or earlier.[74] Some historians maintain that the Egyptians borrowed the use of eunuchs from the Persians. Yet, archeologists have discovered representations of dancing women guarded by eunuchs on the walls of Egyptian tombs dating as early as 4450 BC.[75] Other scholars maintain that the Persians and Babylonians adopted the eunuch way of life only after early contact with the Egyptians. All in all, what we do know is that this practice of castration or the making of *man-made eunuchs* is ancient.

It is fascinating to study the Egyptian, Persian, and Assyrian use of eunuchs because these nations interfaced with the Hebrew nation and are mentioned in the biblical texts. Herodotus, the father of historians, who wrote in the fifth century BC, claimed that it was the Assyrians who were the first to introduce castration for nonreligious reasons into the Near East.[76] Confirmation that the Assyrians did practice castration is found in the book of Isaiah, where the prophet warns King Hezekiah that his sons would be taken away and become eunuchs in the palace of the king of Babylon, which was ruled by the Assyrians in the late eighth century BC.[77]

Eunuchs were considered politically invaluable in that they were usually highly trusted by those they served. According to Xenophon, the Greek historian, Cyrus the Great who ruled Persia in the sixth century BC preferred eunuchs as his officers because he believed that men without wives and children would be loyal to him. This was true even of Cyrus' successor, Darius, who filled all the chief offices of the state with eunuchs.[78] Even though all eunuchs were not used for sexual purposes in these kingdoms, many were. It seems that King Darius III of Persia included both eunuchs and concubines in his harem as did Alexander the Great who defeated Darius.[79]

Because these Eastern nations practiced castration, it has been suggested by some scholars that certain biblical characters serving in the courts of these ancient kingdoms were castrated. For example, the Jewish historian, Josephus, who lived in the first century AD wrote that the prophet Daniel, who was renamed Belteshazzar by the chief eunuch of Babylon, was among the royal Jewish nobility who were castrated by Nebuchadnezzar. The claim by Josephus that Daniel was castrated, however, is not corroborated by the biblical text. Also, Daniel is not identified in the Scriptures as a eunuch although it is clear that there are other eunuchs in the Babylonian kingdom.

In the story of Joseph, a Moslem source[80] as well as the *Midrash Rabbah* assert that Joseph was castrated[81] and that this explains his rise in the house of Potiphar and then in the court of Pharaoh. But, again, there is no mention of this in the biblical text nor is Joseph ever called a eunuch.

Likewise, some people have assumed that Nehemiah, as the cupbearer to Artaxerxes I of Persia was surely a eunuch, just as the cupbearer who was in prison with Joseph in Egypt was a eunuch. It is an interesting proposition since Nehemiah later rose to become the governor of Judea in 445 BC and was a remarkable leader on par with the likes of Daniel and Joseph. However, since there is lack of support in the biblical text itself for these suggestions made by historians, we will disregard them, although it is possible that the biblical text simply ignores the castration of these Hebrew men because it was so disdained.

Historical records indicate that *man-made eunuchs* were used for two primary reasons. First, males were castrated for religious purposes. In ancient Egypt, the castration operation was performed by priests.[82] Similarly, the Chinese referred to castration as the act of entering the priesthood. Eunuchs were even buried separate from their families since they considered themselves priests.[83] A remarkable discovery was made recently at an ancient Yin-dynasty site. Bones found from the Ch'iang people, ancestors of the present-day Tibetans, revealed a piece of bone inscribed with pictographs meant to convey both a penis and cutting. Apparently, this piece of bone was used by the ruler of the Yin when he consulted the gods on whether to make a eunuch of an individual.[84]

Secondly, castration took on a world of its own when castrated males began to gain popularity as servants and chiefs in royal palaces across the East. It seems that, in China, castration began with prisoners as a punishment slightly lesser than decapitation. These prisoners were then placed in the service of the imperial family in order to mostly guard the emperor's concubines and wives. This practice continued throughout Chinese history. Later, a system of how many eunuchs were required in the palace became formalized. For example, the emperor was afforded 3,000 eunuchs, while his sons and daughters were provided with 30 eunuchs each.[85] Of the 3,000 eunuchs in the Emperor's employment, only a few would reach positions of importance and be named the "eunuchs of the presence."[86]

In Turkey, the eunuchs who were over the harems and concubines also had interesting names. For example, in Turkey the eunuchs were both white and black. The white eunuchs would supervise the harem and the head of this group was called the *Supervisor to the Gate*. The black eunuchs were given more important positions. The leader of the black eunuchs was called the chief of servants and officially, "Head of the Blessed Chamber." This was the highest official position a eunuch could attain to in Turkey in service to a Sultan.[87] By the time of the Byzantine period (800–900 AD), the closeness of the eunuchs to the emperor is noted in the highest office of a eunuch being called "The One who lies Beside."[88]

It was really the Assyrians who developed a trade of castrating the children of their conquered and utilizing them in the palace civil service.[89] An interesting note—the eunuchs would keep their severed part or parts, calling them "treasure" and place them in a container that was then kept on a high shelf. In China, this was called the *kao sheng,* meaning high position, and was symbolic of the eunuch attaining a high position.[90] Later on this custom of making *man-made eunuchs* to sell commercially was taken on by the Greeks. The Greek historian, Herodotus, who lived in the fifth century BC, wrote that the Greeks sold their eunuchs at high prices in both Ephesus, an ancient city in Asia Minor, and in Sardis, the capital of Lydia. It was Sardis that retained a reputation as a marketplace for eunuchs.[91]

> Man-made eunuchs were made, whether for religious or commercial purposes, in order to create a new being.

*Man-made eunuchs* were made, whether for religious or commercial purposes, in order to create a new being. The Japanese historian, Taisuke Mitamura, who studied eunuchs in China, describes these man-made eunuchs as "the artificial third sex."[92] Usually, castration just involved the severing of the testicles or even just the wounding of them. But, castration for some males also involved the removal of the penis as well as the testicles. It is no doubt that the castration process caused the castrated males to retain or develop higher voices, more effeminate manners, and soft and hairless bodies. This was especially true if the eunuch had been castrated while young. Those castrated post-puberty were known to still have male hormones which would allow them to feel sexual desire and have the ability to engage in sexual activity.[93] The *hijras*, castrated males who live as women in India, have a religious role derived from Hinduism.[94] Another term used for the *hijras* is "neither man nor woman." Even today in India, it is said that there are males, females, and then *hijras*.

In light of these terms, it is no wonder that Jesus called them exactly what he did call them: *man-made eunuchs*. For whether man-made for religious or commercial purposes, these eunuchs were in a sense artificially created through the means of castration.

As you can imagine, the writers of Scripture opposed this ancient practice of castration. Although the word *eunuch* is not used in the Bible to refer derogatorily to individuals in general, the biblical text does reveal a strong dislike for the practice of castration. For example, in Deuteronomy 23:1, there is a prohibition against any male who has been "emasculated by crushing or cutting" from entering the temple or the assembly of the Lord.

It is interesting that castration was practiced by certain ancient civilizations for two main purposes, both of which were frowned upon by the Hebrew nation. Whether young men were made into eunuchs for religious purposes or castrated for secular reasons such as for punishment or in order to be sold for trade doesn't seem to matter. The idea of man-made eunuchs doesn't seem to originate from God. In fact, it is my view that when Jesus spoke about natural-born eunuchs and then man-made eunuchs, he understood that the first had God's imprint upon them while the second were Satan's attempt at confusing the purpose of God for his eunuch people.

In our introduction to *red-letter eunuchs*, we have seen that Jesus spoke with authority about eunuchs. The first two categories of eunuchs mentioned by Jesus were well-known by his contemporaries. In a later chapter, we will discuss the third category of eunuchs which Jesus instituted. However, for now, it is clear that Jesus' first category of eunuchs is a description of persons today known for their same-sex orientation. Now it is important for us to turn our attention back to the Scriptures in order to see if Jesus' words about eunuchs in Matthew 19:12 are confirmed by the remainder of Scripture. Was Jesus, in fact, teaching about two categories of eunuchs known to exist in the biblical historical record? If so, then we could discover natural-born eunuchs or homosexuals in the Bible.

# 5

## COME OUT, COME OUT, WHEREVER YOU ARE

"For this is what the Lord says: 'To the eunuchs who keep my Sabbaths, who choose what pleases me and hold fast to my covenant— to them I will give within my temple and its walls a memorial and a name….'" ~Isaiah 56:4-5a

In our study so far of *red-letter eunuchs,* based on Jesus' words in Matthew 19, we have seen that the word *eunuch* is significant. The term *eunuch* is a treasure trove because it provides for us a biblical term referencing sexual orientation. Specifically, Jesus' description of *"eunuchs born thus from their mother's womb"* parallels what we know today to be homosexuals. We have seen that Jesus' words about the two known categories of eunuchs are corroborated by extra-biblical writings.

However, just as the extra-biblical writings both confirmed and clarified Jesus' words about eunuchs, it is important for the whole Bible to do so. It is important to see if man-made eunuchs are identified in the Bible. We also need to ask ourselves if natural-born eunuchs, or people of homosexual orientation are identified in the Bible. If they are, then this will only help us understand more fully how God views homosexuals and to know their special purpose in the world.

Since the Bible does not clearly describe each eunuch as either *natural-born* or *man-made*, outside of Jesus' words in Matthew 19:12, we will have to determine what type of eunuch is being referred to as best we can. The distinction can be made, however, by whether the eunuch is said to be in covenant with God or participating in worship at the temple. The reason for this is that castrated eunuchs (man-made) were banned from the temple and were not permitted to be participants of Hebrew religious life.

> The term eunuch is a treasure trove because it provides for us a biblical term referencing sexual orientation. Specifically, Jesus' description of "eunuchs born thus from their mother's womb" parallels what we know today to be homosexuals.

As we turn our attention to how eunuchs are described in the Bible, it becomes apparent that eunuchs are associated with a variety of roles and positions in the ancient world. At first glance, it seems that eunuchs were found to be in the employment of pagan kings and queens. There are eunuchs that served at the pleasure of the King—as in the eunuchs who helped Esther, Joseph, and Daniel.[95] The eunuchs mentioned in these biblical accounts are bakers, cupbearers, doorkeepers, personal assistants to the Pharaoh, high officials in the royal palace, and keepers of the harem. Many people are surprised to discover that eunuchs served in the military. Yet, Genesis 37:36 and 39:1 identifies Potiphar as a *saris*, and he is the captain of Pharaoh's guard. The Scriptures mention that Potiphar is a married *saris* which is unusual. That could explain why his wife was after Joseph.

An interesting explanation of Potiphar's situation is provided by Philo of Alexandria (20 BC-AD 40) in his comments on Genesis 38.[96] Philo acknowledged that Potiphar was a eunuch who happened to be married to a woman. He believed that Potiphar had the *organs of generation* meaning that he was not a castrated male. What this means is that a contemporary of Jesus also understood that not all eunuchs were castrated males. In fact, Philo describes Potiphar specifically as a natural eunuch. What did a natural eunuch mean for Philo? Well, he goes on to discuss Potiphar as being "deprived of all the power requisite for generating." By this, we can understand that Potiphar was either impotent, disinterested in women, or perhaps impotent because he was disinterested in women. He ends by commenting on how a eunuch cohabitating with a wife is an unnatural thing. In this discussion of Potiphar, what we see is that Philo understood natural eunuchs, or Jesus' first category of eunuchs, to be non-castrated males.

All of these eunuchs mentioned thus far served pagan leaders in ancient biblical history. Another surprising discovery for many people is the fact that eunuchs in the Bible also served in the palaces of the Hebrew kings and queens. In 1 Samuel 8:15, the prophet Samuel is trying to discourage the people of Israel from desiring a king to oversee them which was in keeping with all the other nations. He tells them that a king would "…take a tenth of your grain and of your vintage and give it to his officers [saris] and attendants."[97] (NKJV) Here the prophet Samuel is speaking for God and the implication is that it was understood that eunuchs served in kings' palaces.

If we take a good look at the Scriptures, we find that there are eunuchs who served in the palaces of Israel and Judah. In 1 Kings 22:9 and again in 2 Chronicles 18:8, we are told that King Ahab called a eunuch to go fetch the prophet Micaiah so he could prophesy for both he and King Jehoshaphat, the King of Judah. Also, it is interesting that it was two or three eunuchs who threw Jezebel, the wicked queen, out of a window to her death.[98] You have to remember here that, although Jezebel was wicked, she was nevertheless the wife of King Ahab who was the King of Israel. Then, there is the eunuch that is charged by the King of Israel to take care of the Shunammite woman and make sure she receives her land back after the seven years of famine are over.[99] And, one of my favorite stories is about the eunuch who saved Jeremiah from the dungeon. This man had great influence with the king resulting in Jeremiah's life being saved.[100] Then later during the time of the fall of Jerusalem, we are told that the Babylonians captured a eunuch who was in charge of the fighting men. They also captured other eunuchs who served the King in various capacities.[101]

Now, for the most part the many references to eunuchs in the Bible do not specifically indicate whether the eunuchs are *natural-born eunuchs* or *man-made eunuchs*. Most people have assumed that any reference to a eunuch or *saris* in the Bible is generally a reference to a castrated male. However, I would like for you to see how this type of assumption is incorrect based upon the Scriptures themselves.

> These natural-born eunuchs are depicted as people in covenant with God and favored by God. They are biblical examples of what we know today to be homosexual believers.

The fact is Jesus knew what he was talking about when he described different types of eunuchs. When Jesus mentioned *natural-born eunuchs* and then *man-made eunuchs*, he provided for us an acknowledgment of their existence. The Scriptures bear him out because we are going to now take a look at five biblical passages which portray what can only be references to non-castrated eunuchs.[102] These natural-born eunuchs are depicted as people in covenant with God and favored by God. They are biblical examples of what we know today to be homosexual believers.

Let's begin with the eunuchs who served the great king David. A list of leaders who served King David is provided for us in 1 Chronicles 28. In this passage of Scripture, these leaders are invited to King David's speech about the building of the temple under his son Solomon. It is the end of David's life, and he wanted to make sure that all of his leaders would support his son in building the temple that he had envisioned. So, 1 Chronicles 28:1 gives us a list of people that were gathered to hear King David's speech:

"David summoned all the officials of Israel to assemble at Jerusalem: the officers over the tribes, the commanders of the divisions in the service of the king, the commanders of thousands and commanders of hundreds, and the officials in charge of all the king and his sons, together with the palace officials [#5631, Saris], the mighty men and all the brave warriors."[103]

King David employed many eunuchs and they were important enough in status to be called to his final address as king. Now, in case you might be thinking that these eunuchs were possibly castrated or non-Hebrew males, you need to keep reading. We are told that after David's speech to his many leaders, which included eunuchs, he then worshiped the Lord with them as it states in 1 Chronicles 29:20-22a:

Then David said to the whole assembly, 'Praise the Lord your God.' So they all praised the Lord, the God of their fathers; they bowed low and fell prostrate before the Lord and the king. The next day they made sacrifices to the Lord and presented burnt offerings to him: a thousand bulls, a thousand rams and a thousand male lambs, together with their drink offerings, and other sacrifices in abundance for all Israel. They ate and drank with great joy in the presence of the Lord that day.

It might amaze you to see how this passage confirms that these eunuchs who are in King David's service are indeed natural-born eunuchs. The fact that they "praised the Lord, the God of their fathers" is very telling. It means that King David's eunuchs were Hebrew men as well as worshipers of the Lord. These natural-born eunuchs must have been in covenant with God if they were found worshiping God together with the king! This is a beautiful picture for people of same-sex orientation to see because for too long they have been excluded from the public worship of God in the Church.

What we find as we study the topic of eunuchs in the Bible is that there is generally no condemnation toward natural-born eunuchs. It is also remarkable that the Scriptures never seem to mention a eunuch and castration together. It is only implied in Isaiah's prophecy to King Hezekiah when he states that the Babylonians will take some of Hezekiah's own flesh and blood and they will become eunuchs in the palace of the King of Babylon.[104] Since the Babylonians were known to castrate their prisoners, it is certain that this reference is about the "making of eunuchs" through castration as punishment. But, outside of these references to man-made eunuchs or to castration, there is no hint of condescension toward eunuchs found in God's word.

Let me emphasize here that the participation of eunuchs in the public worship of God, as we just saw in 1 Chronicles 29, would not have been possible if they had been castrated males or males with some type of deformity. The Law of Moses prohibited this in Deuteronomy 23:1. It clearly says:

> "He that is wounded in the stones, or hath his privy member cut off, shall not enter into the congregation of the Lord."[105] (King James Version)

In other words, the Law of Moses prohibited castration. Castration was a practice that many ancient civilizations performed, including some of the nations surrounding the Hebrews. In addition, Leviticus 21:20 prohibits anyone from entering the priesthood if they "…hath his stones broken."[106] Finally, even deformed, cut, or wounded animals could not be given as sacrifices to God according to Leviticus 22:24.

To be sure, the Law of Moses prohibited castrated males from entering the temple and from participating in the religious culture of the Hebrew nation. But, in fact, the Bible also reveals to us that there were *natural-born eunuchs* who were in covenant with God and who participated fully in the worship of God. Surprised? Well, let's take a look at a few more examples of what Jesus referred to when he talked about *natural-born eunuchs*.

Another fascinating reference to a *natural-born eunuch* is found in 2 Kings 23:11. During the reign of the reformer, King Josiah, this one eunuch remains untouched during the whole time when King Josiah is removing the idolatrous people from the temple and the city of Jerusalem. Second Kings 23 explains how King Josiah removes the idolatrous priests, the shrine prostitutes (*qadesh*),[107] and those who burned incense to Baal. He also removes the high places as well as anything dedicated to pagan gods like the Asherah pole, and the chariots and horses dedicated to the sun god. However, there is a eunuch at the temple who is not removed or even touched by King Josiah. In 2 Kings 23:11, we are given not only a description of this important eunuch, but we are also told where he resides.

> Many gays and lesbians today would love to be able to fulfill the call of God upon their lives and serve God just as Nathan-Melech did thousands of years ago.

"He [Josiah] removed from the entrance to the temple of the Lord the horses that the Kings of Judah had dedicated to the sun. They were in the court near the room of an official [#5631, saris] named Nathan-Melech. Josiah then burned the chariots dedicated to the sun."[108]

Apparently, this eunuch actually resided at the temple. This verse tells us that this eunuch lived specifically in a room at the entrance to the court to the temple of the Lord. We can know that this is another example of a *natural-born eunuch* in the Scriptures because it is certain that no *man-made eunuch* would have been allowed into the temple of the Lord.

Besides the fact that a eunuch is described as living in the temple, it is impressive that this eunuch's name is given as *Nathan-Melech*. Let's take a moment and break down Nathan-Melech's name so we can get a glimpse of the important status and favor afforded him. Some of the meanings for the name *Nathan* include "to give, add, supply, appoint, ascribe, and assign."[109] The name *Melech* comes from the root word *Malak,* which actually means "to reign, to ascend the throne, to induct into royalty, by implication to counsel, consult, to set up, be made queen, begin to reign or rule."[110] The name of this eunuch implies that he was appointed or assigned by the king to rule and reign in his assignment. This assignment was apparently overseeing the temple. This would explain why he would have lived at the entrance to the temple. His name literally means *Given to the King.*[111] Now, Nathan-Melech would not have been allowed to live at the temple, of all places, if he had been a castrated male, according to the Law of Moses. Therefore, it is certain that he is another example of a natural-born eunuch referred to by Jesus.

Many gays and lesbians today would love to be able to fulfill the call of God upon their lives and serve God just as Nathan-Melech did thousands of years ago. For those who are called to serve in the various ministries of the Church, wouldn't it be wonderful if they were able to do so without any restrictions based upon their sexuality? The truth is, many gays and lesbians who desire to serve God and who love the Church simply are not able to find a place in the Body of Christ where they are accepted and their gifts utilized. It is time that favor is once more restored to Christian gays and lesbians and a new name given to them.

We can find a third reference to natural-born eunuchs who are in covenant with God in Jeremiah 34:19. Here the prophet Jeremiah is prophesying during the time when Nebuchadnezzar, king of Babylon, and his army are fighting against Jerusalem. Apparently, during this time, King Zedekiah, the king of Judah, had established a covenant among all the people of Jerusalem which instructed them to release their Hebrew slaves. The people at first allowed their Hebrew slaves to go free but then they took them back. Jeremiah now has a stinging word from God for these people. The result of their disobedience is that God will hand them over to their enemies. Whom does God address in this rebuke? Jeremiah 34:19-20a tells us who in the following.

"The leaders of Judah and Jerusalem, the court officials
(#5631, Saris), the priests and all the people of the land

who walked between the pieces of the calf, I will hand over to their enemies who seek their lives...."[112] (KJV)

What is important for us to see in this scriptural passage is that the eunuchs are not only included in the leadership of the Hebrew people, but they are more importantly described as in covenant with God. God's word specifically includes the eunuchs as those who had *walked between the pieces of the calf* which refers to the process of entering into a covenant through a blood ceremony. If these eunuchs had been castrated or even somehow deformed at birth, then they would not have been afforded the blessing of being full participants in covenant with God. As you can see, even though this word is a rebuke for the leaders, eunuchs, and priests in Jerusalem, it is also a confirmation that natural-born eunuchs were full participants in the Hebrew religious life. This provides encouragement for gay and lesbian Christians today that they too are to be full participants in the life of the Church.

> God is bringing modern day eunuchs out of exile at this time. God is providing for gays and lesbians their place of calling within their families, their Churches, and in the world.

A fourth example of natural-born eunuchs found to be in covenant with God comes to us after the Babylonian exile, when Jeremiah writes a letter to the exiled Hebrews. Jeremiah 29:1-2 tells us that eunuchs were included in their number.

"This is the text of the letter that the prophet Jeremiah sent from Jerusalem to the surviving elders among the exiles and to the priests, the prophets, and all the other people Nebuchadnezzar had carried into exile from Jerusalem to Babylon. (This was after King Jehoiachin and the queen mother, the court officials [saris, #5631] and the leaders of Judah and Jerusalem, the craftsmen and the artisans had gone into exile from Jerusalem.)"[113]

In this same letter, Jeremiah goes on to encourage the exiles, including the eunuchs, to live life normally and to seek the peace of the city they live in. Jeremiah also provides them with a powerful covenant promise from God in verses 10-14a. This promise is the one that later stirred Daniel to begin making intercession to God to bring the Hebrew nation back to their land. Daniel discerned from Jeremiah's prophecy that God promised to do this after seventy years were completed.

We must realize that Jeremiah 29:10-14a is a covenant promise also given to the *natural-born eunuchs* who are in exile. For, if they had been *man-made eunuchs*, they would certainly not have been included as a covenant people, and the letter would not have been addressed to them. With this in mind, read the promise of God to his covenant people in Jeremiah 29:10-14a.

> This is what the Lord says: 'When seventy years are completed for Babylon, I will come to you and fulfill my gracious promise to bring you back to this place. For I know the plans I have for you,' declares the Lord, 'plans to prosper you and not to harm you, plans to give you hope and a future. Then you will call upon me and come and pray to me, and I will listen to you. You will seek me and find me when you seek me with all your heart. I will be found by you,' declares the Lord, 'and will bring you back from captivity.'

This beautiful promise of God echoes down through the ages to modern-day eunuchs who have perhaps been exiled from their place of life and worship because of their sexuality. God is bringing modern day eunuchs out of exile at this time. God is providing for gays and lesbians their place of calling within their families, their Churches, and in the world.

There is one final eunuch that I would like to point to as an example of a *natural-born eunuch*. This eunuch's story is given to us by the only Gentile writer of the New Testament as recorded in Acts 8:27-39. Luke shares with us a wonderful story of how an Ethiopian eunuch on his way back from Jerusalem experiences salvation in Christ Jesus. What is remarkable about this New Testament account of a eunuch is that it reveals to us how the salvation of this eunuch is of utmost importance to God.

First we are told that an angel of the Lord supernaturally speaks to Philip, the evangelist, and tells him where to meet the eunuch. So, Philip arrives at a desert crossroads where he finds what is only described as an Ethiopian eunuch. This eunuch apparently serves the Queen of Ethiopia as treasurer, no less. Other than this introduction, Luke calls this nameless man a eunuch five more times. It seems to me that the Holy Spirit wanted to highlight this man's *eunuchism* for us because he serves as a biblical model of how God is after modern-day eunuchs or those of same-sex orientation. The bottom line is that this eunuch receives Christ and is baptized in water by the end of his encounter with Philip.

Though the Scriptures do not specifically state that this eunuch is a *natural-born eunuch,* it does seem to be the most honest conclusion we can make. The reason for this is that we are told very simply in Acts 8:27b that, "This man had gone to Jerusalem to worship." This man is described by Luke as an Ethiopian, and at some point in his life he had become a believer and worshiper of God. Perhaps he heard the message of God through some Jews who had been scattered into the nations of the earth. Then he decided to go to Jerusalem to worship. Something similar is described in Acts 2, where on the Day of Pentecost there is a host of people in Jerusalem including, "Jews and converts to Judaism." So, it seems that, in the same way, this eunuch who is a convert makes the long and difficult journey to Jerusalem to worship the Lord in the temple.

However, before going on such a long journey, doesn't it seem logical that this influential eunuch would have inquired if he would have been allowed to worship the God of the Jews in the temple of Jerusalem? I think it seems most likely, if in fact this eunuch would have been a *man-made eunuch.* You see if the Ethiopian eunuch had been a *man-made eunuch,* he would have been banned from the temple according to the Law of Moses. He would not have been able to enter the temple premises at all and would have been forbidden to worship God with the other worshippers. For this reason, I believe it is most certain that this Ethiopian eunuch is another example of a *natural-born eunuch*.

As it is, the Ethiopian eunuch would have had to worship the Lord from the court of the Gentiles because of his nationality. This barrier was one of many in the Jerusalem temple and it specifically kept the Gentile converts from the Jewish believers. At least he would have been able to worship the Lord in Jerusalem at the temple with other Gentiles in the court reserved for them.

This eunuch's encounter with Christ on the road to Ethiopia was evidently as life-changing as Saul's encounter with Christ on the road to Damascus. We can know this by the fact that this natural-born eunuch is credited as being the Father of Christianity for Ethiopia. This account of the Ethiopian eunuch gives us reason to believe that the salvation of gays and lesbians is still of utmost importance to the Lord. We need to make sure that on this side of the cross of Jesus Christ every barrier is removed so every person has the opportunity to receive the joy of their salvation. If the Church will do this, then we will see mighty moves of God's Spirit as modern-day eunuchs fulfill their call to the nations of the world.

An example of a recent modern-day eunuch is found in the life of Lonnie Frisbee, who was one of the key personalities in the Jesus Movement during the 1970s. His story is documented in the 2007 Emmy-nominated film *Frisbee: The Life and Death of a Hippie Preacher* by David di Sabatino. Frisbee was a young hippie who was involved in mysticism and the occult until he encountered Christ surprisingly during an LSD acid trip. As with the Ethiopian eunuch, God's hand was upon him in a great way. Lonnie Frisbee had a vision from God which put a fire in his heart. He saw himself preaching in front of a sea of young people crying out to God. Through a series of events, Lonnie Frisbee was introduced to Chuck Smith, a pastor of a small congregation called Calvary Chapel in Costa Mesa, California. Within a few short months, this Church that had stagnated for seventeen years started to swell to over a thousand members with Lonnie's influence. Hundreds of thousands of young people came to know Christ as savior under his ministry.

From there, Frisbee came to know John Wimber and was invited to speak at his new Church in Yorba Linda called the Vineyard. Frisbee's explosive Spirit-filled ministry greatly impacted the Vineyard as well. By the end of his life, Frisbee was used of God as a key figure in the Jesus Movement and as the spark that ignited two worldwide evangelical denominations. Sadly, he contracted AIDS and passed away in 1993. Once Lonnie's sexuality was revealed, his gifts and influence were discounted by the very ones that he had impacted. The story of Lonnie Frisbee is a story of a modern-day eunuch who did not fully understand his God-given sexuality.

It is time for modern-day eunuchs to understand and recognize their identity in Christ as well as the magnitude of their calling. In the summer of 2007 I went to the Crystal Cathedral in Garden Grove, California, and visited the site where Lonnie Frisbee was laid to rest. I invited several students from our Ministry Training School and a few pastors to go with me. I felt directed by the Holy Spirit to ask God to release the mantle or anointing of Lonnie Frisbee in the earth again. After all, Lonnie Frisbee's life and gifts were not esteemed and valued by his peers when he passed away because of his sexual orientation. So we prayed that the mantle God had placed upon this incredible man, which was lying dormant, would be released upon this next generation. It was a beautiful time of prayer and we blessed Lonnie Frisbee and thanked God for the life of this modern-day eunuch. I pray that God raises up many more modern-day eunuchs in this next generation who will encounter Christ and walk in His power, but who will also have an understanding of their calling, gifts, and uniqueness.

We have now seen four Old Testament examples of natural-born eunuchs and one example provided for us in the New Testament. The Ethiopian eunuch, a gay man, is also the first and only eunuch mentioned in the Scriptures who experiences Christ! All of these natural-born eunuchs are favored by God and also seem to have prestigious leadership positions. They are examples for us of how God views gays and lesbians with favor. They also reveal to us how God desires to use gay and lesbian Christians in positions of influence in the Church and in the world.

It makes sense that when Jesus spoke about "eunuchs born thus from their mother's womb" that he would have understood their biblical history. I also believe that when Jesus spoke about these natural-born eunuchs, he was prophetically opening up the door for gays and lesbians to walk in their intended calling, purpose, and gifting.

Now, in the next chapter we will see how it all begins… in the mother's womb.

# 6

# In My Mother's Womb

"For you created my inmost being; you knit me together in my mother's womb. I praise you because I am fearfully and wonderfully made…." ~Psalm 139:13-14a

God's sovereignty in each of our lives is often unappreciated. We need to be reminded that each of us has the print of our Creator in us. We are God's stamp, God's image. According to the Scriptures, we are knit together in our mother's womb. Each of us is fearfully and wonderfully made by a loving God.

A well-known prophet came to our Church and called me out from the crowd in order to give me a personal word of prophecy from the Lord. He did not know me nor could he have had personal knowledge of my missionary parents. But his prophetic word came forth this way: "The Lord says, when you were born, your parents dedicated you to Me as a baby. You were given over into My care, and it was prayed that you would be raised up as a mighty woman of God." When I heard the beginning of this word of prophecy I knew that I could receive the rest of it because it was a confirmation of what I knew to be true. My parents had indeed dedicated me to the Lord and prayed that God would use me mightily.

As wonderful as it is to know that we have been dedicated to God once we are born, it is even more astounding to know that God has been intricately involved in our lives from our mother's womb. Psalm 139:13-16 speaks to us about the depths of God's sovereignty and creativity in forming each individual in the womb.

> As wonderful as it is to know that we have been dedicated to God once we are born, it is even more astounding to know that God has been intricately involved in our lives from our mother's womb.

"For you created my inmost being; you knit me together in my mother's womb. I praise you because I am fearfully and wonderfully made; your works are wonderful, I know that full well. My frame was not hidden from you when I was made in the secret place. When I was woven together in the depths of the earth, your eyes saw my unformed body. All the days ordained for me were written in your book before one of them came to be."

God has lovingly formed each one of us—spirit, soul, and body—while in our mothers' wombs. It is always fun to see a little baby's resemblance to a parent or family member. And within a few short hours, days, or weeks it becomes apparent that every child has a distinct personality, although oftentimes identical to a parent or family member. This is the reason that people make comments like, "Little Bobby has Grandpa's red hair," or "Susie is the spitting image of her mother." Even while we were concealed in the darkness of the womb, or in *the depths of the earth*, God nevertheless saw every part being woven together. Ultimately, the most important aspect or characteristic that we all carry is that we are "made in the image of God."

Psalm 139:13-16 speaks clearly about two very different parts of the individual and how they are formed by God. First, it says in verse 13 that God creates the *inmost being* which is knit together in the mother's womb. The Hebrew word translated as inmost being is *Kilyah,* which can mean kidneys, or when used figuratively, it means the seat of emotions and affections.[114] Sometimes this word is translated into English in the Bible variously as spirit, mind, or heart. It is a reference to the soul and the very inner being of an individual. *The New Bible Commentary* by Eerdmans states that the Hebrew word *Kilyah* clearly refers to the psychological aspect of a human being.[115] With this in mind, it is plain to see that the area of the soul that is the seat of emotions and affections is formed in the womb. The inner being is therefore comprised of important aspects of one's personhood such as one's mind, emotions, and personality. Another important psychological component of the inner being, I believe, is one's sexuality. It is wonderful that all of the psychological characteristics of an individual are knitted perfectly together, making the individual whole and complete.

> Nothing about an individual's physicality, emotions, mind, spirit, or even sexuality is hidden from the Lord. Rather, God knows you and has a destiny for your life—a destiny which is already written down in heaven.

Secondly, God's word indicates that the physical form of an individual is also created in the womb. The outer physicality of the human being is referred to throughout the Bible as clay, dust, a tent, or a jar. It is the outer shell which contains the true self of the individual made up of the spirit and soul. Our spirits are eternal. The outer shell of the human being is temporal. These verses let us know that the physical form of the human being is also created in the womb.

This beautiful psalm describes how each human being is sovereignly formed, created, knitted, and woven together, all of this taking place in the mother's womb. The idea that the psalm portrays is that God is aware and acquainted with every aspect of every individual. Nothing about an individual's physicality, emotions, mind, spirit, or even sexuality is hidden from the Lord. Rather, God knows you and has a destiny for your life—a destiny which is already written down in heaven. David, the psalmist, praised the Lord in this song because of God's works. He said that human beings are fearfully and wonderfully made. We are God's crowning achievement. We are the ones made in the image of the Creator.

You and I are fearfully and wonderfully made! To be *fearfully* made simply has the meaning of awe and reverence.[116] Whenever I look at a little baby's hand or fingertips, I am reminded of how intricately we are made. Each of us is God's handiwork. To be *wonderfully* made carries the meaning of being distinct, marked out, separated, distinguished, and set apart.[117] God doesn't mind at all that human beings are all created distinctly and separately. So you see, you don't have to worry if your personality, skills, talents, physical shape, or even sexuality are different from everybody else's. There is no mold that is used and then reused when it comes to God's handiwork. Each one of us is as unique as our very fingerprints. Since we are fearfully and wonderfully made we can accept ourselves, love ourselves, and love our Creator.

We need to understand that even God's word affirms diversity in humanity. To be wonderfully made means to be distinct, set apart, marked out, and distinguished. God is the one that forms every human being and each have God's stamp of approval. And we have seen that this forming and knitting together of the human being begins in the mother's womb. This confirms the words of Jesus when he said there are "eunuchs who were born thus from their mother's womb."[118] We have already seen that these natural-born eunuchs are the equivalent of modern-day gays and lesbians. All of God's word informs us, and we should listen to it so we can love and accept all of God's handiwork.

To compliment what God's word implies regarding the formation of sexuality and its origins in the womb are various studies. Over the last few years, much research has been accomplished on the topic of homosexuality within the fields of psychology, sociology, and even in biology. A discussion has developed in these fields regarding the origins of sexuality and of course, of homosexuality. Interestingly enough, the first discussion of innate versus acquired homosexuality was first presented by Aristotle.[119] I guess you could say this has been a topic of interest to people for quite some time.

Although research on homosexuality in the area of biology is over one-hundred years old,[120] there has been much enthusiasm in the last twenty to thirty years over some published findings. Some of the biological research that has taken place in the last few decades has centered on studies on the brain, hormones, and genetics. It is interesting to me that the word genetics is derived from the ancient Greek word *genetikos* which comes from the word *genesis,* meaning origin. The study of genetics is a biological discipline regarding heredity. Wouldn't it be just like God to have the secrets of sexuality simply encoded within human genes as they are knit together in the womb? Although the biological research on homosexuality is fairly new, what seems clear is that prenatal events have much to do with sexuality.

To date, the research findings point to at least a partly biological explanation for sexual orientation.[121] Some of the research has uncovered brain, genetic, and even prenatal findings that provide clues to sexual orientation. One of the most notable brain findings was made in 1991, by neuroscientist, Simon LeVay, when he discovered that the brain's hypothalamus in heterosexual men was larger than that of heterosexual women and homosexual men. The hypothalamus is known as the seat of emotions and sexual drives for humans. LeVay found that the hypothalamus INAH 3, a particular cluster of cells in the forefront of the hypothalamus, was twice the volume in heterosexual men than in homosexual men. According to LeVay, it is unclear whether the brain anatomy differences between these populations of people represent a cause or a result of homosexuality.[122] At the time, LeVay's findings caused quite a stir, particularly in the United States.

An earlier study on the hypothalamus was first published in 1985, in *Science* when Professor D. F. Swaab, a neurobiologist at the University of Amsterdam, and another colleague, E. Fliers, published a report revealing that a region of the hypothalamus was showing

> To date, the research findings point to at least a partly biological explanation for sexual orientation.

different structures in females and males.[123] Later in 1990, Professor Swaab and another colleague, M.A. Hofman, found a particular nucleus in the hypothalamus, the suprachiasmatic nucleus, to be larger in homosexual men than in heterosexual men.[124] This is a different part of the hypothalamus than what was later described by LeVay in 1991.

Another significant brain study reported in 1992, by two neurobiologists, Laura Allen and Roger Gorski from the Laboratory of Neuroendocrinology at the University of California at Los Angeles, confirmed that brain anatomy influences sexual orientation.[125] They discovered that a section of the anterior commissure is one-third larger in homosexual men than in heterosexual men. The anterior commissure is a group of fibers lying adjacent to the hypothalamus and interconnecting the temporal lobes of the brain. These brain fibers connect right and left hemispheres and seem to indicate that homosexual men lean toward having female-typical neuroanatomy. Although these studies are just the tip of the iceberg when it comes to understanding a correlation between the brain and sexuality, what these studies do point to is the fact that some brain anatomical differences seem to be related to sexual orientation.

About a year later, in July 1993, a major biological discovery in the area of genetics caused a tremendous commotion. I still have the *Wall Street Journal,* dated July 16, 1993, which had the article entitled, "Research Points Toward a 'Gay' Gene." The article described the findings of a research team (Hamer, Hu, Magnuson, Hu, and Pattatucci) studying the development of cancers in people infected with the HIV virus at the Laboratory of Biochemistry at the National Cancer Institute in Bethesda, Maryland. They published a study in *Science* when they discovered a gene on the long arm of the X-chromosome in males that is correlated to homosexual orientation.[126] The research centered on blood samples from men who self-identified as homosexuals and their male relatives. These researchers concluded that homosexuality was more likely transmitted genetically through mothers since men derive their single X-chromosome from their mothers.

A later genetic study, published in 2005, was the first to research the entire human genome in an effort to find determinants of male sexual orientation.[127] Previous studies had only focused on the X chromosome while this study examined the X chromosome along with all twenty-two pairs of non-sex chromosomes. It sampled 456 individuals from 146 unrelated families of which 137 families had two gay brothers and nine families had three gay brothers. The result of the study was the discovery that there is not just one "gay gene." These researchers found that gay brothers in the study shared stretches of DNA on three different chromosomes—chromosomes seven, eight, and ten.

Interestingly enough, the highlighted chromosome seven is related to the development of the hypothalamic suprachiasmatic nucleus.[128] This correlates with the Swaab and Hofman 1990 study which found the suprachiasmatic nucleus enlarged in homosexual men. Also, chromosome ten seems to have a maternal origin which correlates with various studies showing the X chromosome's relationship to male homosexual orientation and the fact that men derive their X chromosome from their mothers. Although inconclusive at this time, the study reveals that genes do play a part in determining sexual orientation.

Finally, another important area of biological research informing the discussion on the origins of homosexual orientation has focused on the area of prenatal hormones. A groundbreaking theory on prenatal events determining sexuality was proposed by Lee Ellis and M. Ashley Ames in 1987, when they found that the process of determining sexual orientation is fundamentally the same for all mammals.[129] They write:

> "According to the present theory, sexual orientation in all mammals is primarily determined by the degree to which the nervous system is exposed to testosterone, its metabolite estradiol, and to certain other sex hormones while neuro-organization is taking place. … For humans, sexual orientation appears to be primarily determined roughly between the middle of the second and the end of the fifth month of gestation (Ehrhardt et al., 1984, p. 459)."[130]

According to Lee Ellis and M. Ashley Ames, there are genetic, hormonal, neurological, and environmental factors that all take place prior to birth which largely determine sexual orientation, although sexual orientation is not activated until puberty or stabilized until early adulthood.

The 1996 discovery by Ray Blanchard and Anthony Bogaert of the fraternal birth-order effect is related to the prenatal biological research. These researchers found that there is a fraternal birth-order effect which is related to a male child's sexual orientation development.[131] Apparently, a mother provides a prenatal environment that fosters homosexuality in younger sons. It was found in this study that a boy's chance of growing up to be homosexual increases by a third with each additional brother that precedes him. There does not seem to be any corresponding effect for lesbians who have older sisters.

In 2001, Ray Blanchard and L. Ellis hypothesized that a mother's exposure to proteins was related to the fraternal birth-order effect.[132] It is thought that a mother carrying her first son has little exposure to her son's proteins due to the placenta. However, after the delivery, there is a mixing of the mother's blood with the son's blood, causing the mother's immune system to be exposed to the son's proteins, including proteins encoded on her son's Y chromosome. If the mother then has an immune response to these proteins, then other sons she carries would be exposed to maternal antibodies directed against these male-specific proteins.

The fraternal birth-order effect has gained quite a bit of notoriety in the last few years. But, there is still much more to be learned when it comes to sexual orientation and prenatal events. For example, it was a surprise when researcher Ray Blanchard discovered that the fraternal birth-order effect only seems to matter in cases where the younger son is right- handed.[133] Apparently, where men are left-handed, there is no difference in the incidence of homosexuality regardless of the number of brothers a left-handed male may have. So, as you can see, there is still much more to be discovered.

All of the biological research to date has unearthed numerous unanswered questions regarding the causality of homosexuality. Yet, although sexual orientation seems to be determined by a combination of many factors, it is becoming more and more clear that the origins of sexuality is indeed determined in the womb. This correlates not only with much modern research but also with the words of Jesus that there are "eunuchs who were born thus from their mother's womb."

There is a shift in public sentiment regarding sexuality due to the consistent findings pointing toward some degree of biological explanation for sexuality. For example, a 2002 Gallup study revealed that 40 percent of the American public saw homosexuality as "something a person is born with" as opposed to 13 percent in 1977.[134] Also, most psychiatrists now believe that sexual orientation is a predisposition.[135] In August 2009, the American Psychological Association adopted a resolution on a 125-to-4 vote based upon a two year study that opposed "reparative therapy" which seeks to change sexual orientation. Instead, the APA urged therapists to consider other options such as celibacy or switching Churches for helping clients.[136]

For too long, many Christians have wondered how it is that there could be sexual diversity within humanity. This lack of knowledge has caused much hurt and misunderstanding for young gay, lesbian, bisexual, and transgender people. Rejecting truth as Christians, even if it is newly acquired, can have detrimental effects upon others and cause people to reject Christianity. I like how Francis A. Schaeffer, Christian philosopher and theologian, understood that anything true had to have its origins in God. He was known by this statement: "All truth is God's truth."

> Rejecting truth as Christians, even if it is newly acquired, can have detrimental effects upon others and cause people to reject Christianity.

Many years ago the Catholic Church rejected the notion that all the planets, including the earth, revolve around the sun. This fact that we understand today as truth was considered heretical in 1632, when Galileo, a scientist and a Christian, supported it. Galileo refused to recant his support of this fifteenth century idea of Copernicus. Therefore, Galileo was branded a heretic and was placed under house arrest for the rest of his life. Almost beyond belief, it took 359 years, or until 1992,

67

for Pope John Paul II to finally admit that the Catholic Church had been in the wrong and offer an apology.[137] This is a perfect example of what can happen as Christians when we refuse to allow new truth to inform us and the Bible.

The fact is the whole universe reflects some aspect of who God is. There is a song of praise being sung in the heavens and in the seas. The mountains and the valleys are all His idea. The heavens portray the gospel story from the virgin to the Lion. Everything that God has made must praise the Lord! Yet, in the midst of the grandeur and diversity of God's handiwork, there is also individuality and familiarity. God knows everyone by name.

Be assured that God knew you in the womb and He is fully familiar with who you are now. In the language of the East, this means that God knows your name.

# 7

# A BETTER NAME

"The nations will see your righteousness, and all kings your glory; you
will be called by a new name that the mouth of the Lord will bestow."
~Isaiah 62:2 (NIV)

Names are important. The Bible gives us some good advice
about names in Proverbs 22:1. It says, "A good name is more
desirable than great riches; to be esteemed is better than silver or gold."

In the ancient East, names were selected very carefully because they
were to reveal the character or destiny of the name bearer. I love the
fact that often in the Bible we see God changing someone's name out
of love for the individual. In some instances, God would change a name
in order to give someone a better or more fitting name, or perhaps to
remove the stigma of a character flaw in the person. This was the case
with Jacob. His name meant *deceiver* and he certainly lived up to his
name. So, God changed his name to *Israel*, which means *prince*.

69

In the same way, it is God's desire for eunuchs to have a good name. When Jesus used the term *eunuch* in Matthew 19:12, he didn't change the name at all, but Jesus did redeem it. The name, once respected, was no longer held in high regard at the time. It seems that a growing contempt for eunuchs had developed alongside the expansion of man-made eunuchs. So, when Jesus spoke about eunuchs in front of an audience of religious leaders and disciples, he must have shocked them. But, whatever came from Jesus' lips carried authority and brought life. So, when Jesus spoke the name *eunuch* in front of his peers, he changed the reputation associated with the name and extended grace to all eunuchs.

Jesus' words were divinely inspired and they echoed what the prophet Isaiah had spoken approximately 700 years prior. In Isaiah 56:4-5, we find a wonderful prophecy of hope given to eunuchs. Here God speaks through his prophet and commands a promise that extends to us today. Isaiah prophesied:

> So, when Jesus spoke the name eunuch in front of his peers, he changed the reputation associated with the name and extended grace to all eunuchs.

> "For thus says the Lord: 'To the eunuchs who keep My Sabbaths, and choose what pleases me, and hold fast my covenant, even to them I will give in my house and within my walls, a place and a name better than that of sons and daughters; I will give them an everlasting name that shall not be cut off.'"[138] (NKJV)

This wonderful promise of God to eunuchs is twofold: First, it states that eunuchs will be given a place in God's house. God's house today is the Church or the family of God. It also says that eunuchs will have a name better than sons and daughters. This promise is addressed to eunuchs who have a specific commitment and devotion to the Lord. It seems to me that Jesus must have had Isaiah's prophecy in mind when he spoke about eunuchs who would choose to be eunuchs for the sake of the kingdom of heaven. So, eunuchs who choose to commit themselves to God are promised a place in God's house and a better name.

One means of obtaining a better name is by having a better position. Apparently, God wants to give to eunuchs a whole new position. This position is found in God's house.

There are two aspects of the promise given to eunuchs that I would like to highlight because they are only given to eunuchs.

### Eunuchs will be given a place in God's house

First of all, God promises that eunuchs will be given within God's house a *place*. This is a very important promise because to this day, many nations have been included in the Church worldwide while many gays and lesbians are still excluded. The word *place* in the Hebrew is the word *yad,* which usually means hand.[139] However, at times, this word is translated differently because of the context of the verse. In this case, *yad* has the meaning of "a monument, a trophy, as in a hand which points and marks."[140]

What strikes me about this part of the promise of God to eunuchs is that it emphasizes the fact that God has marked a place especially for eunuchs in His temple. I see it like a big "X" which marks the place that only eunuchs will occupy within God's temple or the modern-day Church. No other people group will be able to take this particular place because it is reserved by the Most High God for His eunuchs. Picture a roped off area in the worldwide Church and then begin to see how God is inviting His gay and lesbian children to enter into what has been reserved for them. Gays and lesbians are a people who are in every nation in the world. The worldwide Church needs to get ready to receive all of God's gay and lesbian children in the place that has been set apart for them.

> I see it like a big "X" which marks the place that only eunuchs will occupy within God's temple or the modern-day Church.

This promise of God is still taking place today as God sovereignly invites modern-day eunuchs to find their place in God's house. In the New

Testament, the temple becomes the Church in one of its applications. I love the way the apostle Paul writes about all believers coming together to form God's household and God's temple in Ephesians 2:19-22:

> "Consequently, you are no longer foreigners and aliens, but fellow citizens with God's people and members of God's household, built on the foundation of the apostles and prophets, with Christ Jesus himself as the chief cornerstone. In Him the whole building is joined together and rises to become a holy temple in the Lord. And in Him you too are being built together to become a dwelling in which God lives by His Spirit."

Isn't it wonderful that God has promised that the doors of the Church will be opened so that eunuchs can become members of God's household? Those who have been excluded and rejected will find that there is a place where they belong and it is in the family of God. I have met countless thousands of gays and lesbians who at one time were full participants in the Church, but once their sexuality became known either to themselves or to the Church, they no longer felt welcomed or included. Some were even painfully kicked out of the Church and at times, in a public way. The day is coming when this will no longer be the case according to God's promise.

When gays and lesbians do find their rightful place in the Church, it will be a day of great advancement for the Church. Can you imagine what Churches would be like with the gifts of gays and lesbians welcomed and used? Presently, there are gays and lesbians who stay in the Church, but because of the fear of having their sexuality discovered, they hide their gifts. These gays and lesbians really live in the back pews and shadows of ministries and organizations. Others have Church leaders who are suspicious of them, and because of this, they are never really given the opportunity to use their gifts. Then, think about all of the gays and lesbians who have walked out of Church doors because they could not live a double life or live under the pressure of a lie. Such stories represent innumerable gifts which are lying dormant today. These stories represent destinies that are yet to be fulfilled. The doors of the Church will be opened up to those that have been rejected and denied their place when true apostles and prophets lay a right foundation. So watch as God brings in and gathers together his outcast eunuchs.

Jesus Himself was very familiar with the full prophecy of Isaiah found in Isaiah 56. Let's take a look at the remainder of the prophecy which Isaiah shared regarding eunuchs and foreigners in Isaiah 56:7-8.

> "These I will bring to my holy mountain and give them joy in my house of prayer. Their burnt offerings and sacrifices will be accepted on my altar; for my house will be called a house of prayer for all nations. The Sovereign Lord declares—he who gathers the exiles of Israel: 'I will gather still others to them besides those already gathered.'"

Jesus echoed this prophecy when he spoke about other sheep that he would gather together. In John 10:16, Jesus spoke these beautiful words of inclusion:

> "I have other sheep that are not of this sheep pen. I must bring them also. They too will listen to my voice, and there shall be one flock and one shepherd."

## Eunuchs will be given a better name

Eunuchs have also been promised a *better* name. The word "better" in this prophecy is a translation of the Hebrew word *towb,* which basically means "good."[141] It is wonderful that God announced many years ago that eunuchs would have a good name. In order for you to really get the gist of how God feels about eunuchs, let me share with you a few more meanings attached to this Hebrew word *towb. The Strong's Exhaustive Concordance of the Bible* states that this word can be defined as: "beautiful, best, better, bountiful, cheerful, at ease, fair, favor, fine, glad, good, graciously, joyful, kindness, loving, mercy, pleasant, prosperity, precious, wealth, (be) well (favored)."[142] It seems that it is in the heart of God to make sure that eunuchs enjoy a good name and great favor. One day, gays and lesbians are going to have a well-favored, precious, and good name because God will see that His promise is accomplished.

However, it is important to note that the Bible translators have all translated the Hebrew word *towb* as "better" for this verse because of the context. The name that God has given to eunuchs is compared in this verse to the name of sons and daughters. Eunuchs are to have a name that is *better* than that of sons and daughters. This means that not only does God promise to include eunuchs into his house or family, but also eunuchs are to be given a particular name that is better than the name of sons and daughters. What could this name be?

We know that in the Church all of God's children are called sons and daughters of God. We are all a part of the family of God through adoption. Paul writes in Galatians 3:26-29 how all believers belong in the family of God and that the walls of division that existed before are removed.

> "You are all sons [and daughters] of God through faith in Christ Jesus, for all of you who were baptized into Christ have clothed yourselves with Christ. There is neither Jew nor Greek, slave nor free, male nor female, for you are all one in Christ Jesus. If you belong to Christ, then you are Abraham's seed, and heirs according to the promise."

In effect, God has given every believer a place in the Church and all are either sons or daughters of God. Yet, Isaiah's prophecy specifically states that eunuchs would be given a name that is better than that of sons and daughters. So, what type of name is better than that of sons and daughters?

I believe that for eunuchs who choose to be in covenant with God, there is a name given which is a term of endearment. God has given eunuchs who delight in the Lord a cherished name.

Years ago, I was studying the promise of God to eunuchs in Isaiah 56, and began to wonder about this name. After all, it is a privilege to be a child of God; to be a part of God's family. So, what could this name be? I began to ask the Holy Spirit to show me what this promise of God means for gays and lesbians today. One morning I woke up at three in the morning with the Holy Spirit impressing upon my heart the name *Beloved*. Immediately I felt the Holy Spirit speak to my heart that this was the name given by God to the eunuch nation. I thought it was a beautiful name! And, to be sure, it certainly is a new name. Gays and lesbians today have been called many things by family members, Church members, and by society. However, I'm not sure that gay and lesbian believers have understood the name that has been given to them by God. *Beloved* is a term of endearment. It is a name to be cherished because it is a name given to those who are willing to enter into intimacy with the Lord.

> God is saying to gays and lesbians who have been excluded and rejected in the past, that there is a special place and a special name reserved for them. For those who can accept it, the new name for modern-day eunuchs is Beloved.

I asked the Holy Spirit to give me a scriptural understanding for this better name given to modern day eunuchs. The Holy Spirit impressed upon my heart how the apostle John referred to himself as the *beloved* disciple. John wrote in the Gospel of John how he was the disciple whom Jesus loved five different times.[143] It seems that from the twelve disciples, Jesus selected an inner circle with Peter, James, and John. Yet, out of the three disciples who were the closest to Jesus, apparently, He loved John the most. It is John who leans his head against the Master's breast. This position of closeness and intimacy is not a hidden position either. Later on it is the risen Christ who appears to this same apostle while he is imprisoned on the island of Patmos. John is given a breadth of revelation that is still a source of blessing to the Church today.

Today, I believe that God is looking for a eunuch people who will find their position within God's family and enter into a relationship of intimacy with the Lord. God is saying to gays and lesbians who have been excluded and rejected in the past, that there is a special place and a special name reserved for them. For those who can accept it, the new name for modern-day eunuchs is *Beloved*. *Beloved* are those gays and lesbians who have been destined to and who also choose to be in covenant with God and receive their place and new name in the kingdom of God.

Many in the Church are seeking power, but few are seeking God's face. God has a special position reserved for his chosen eunuchs who will devote themselves to Him. He desires a relationship of intimacy with his *Beloved* so that His heart is known. This will release special insight, revelation, and understanding for life and ministry.

So, if you are gay or lesbian, these questions are for you:

"Will you choose to commit yourself to God?"

"Are you willing to please God and know His heart?"

"Will you listen as He calls you by a new name?"

# 8

# THE POWER OF A LIE

"… He was a murderer from the beginning, not holding to the truth, for there is no truth in him. When he lies, he speaks his native language, for he is a liar and the father of lies." ~John 8:44

There is no doubt that true freedom comes from knowing Jesus Christ as Savior. But living a life of true freedom can be challenging for many gay, lesbian, bisexual, and transgender people. This is especially true when parts of society and the Christian Church struggle to understand the diversity of human sexuality. For Christians, we are committed to allowing God's word to be our guide. What must not be neglected, however, when we approach God's word, is the role of the Holy Spirit in bringing understanding. Jesus described the Holy Spirit to his disciples as the *Spirit of Truth*, and the one who would teach us all things and guide us into all truth.[144] The by-product of the Holy Spirit illuminating God's word for us is that ultimately freedom is experienced.

"Now the Lord is the Spirit, and where the Spirit of the Lord is, there is freedom."[145]

It has been a joy to see many gay and lesbian people come to a saving knowledge of Christ Jesus, and then watch them find freedom as the Spirit of God illuminates God's word to them.

Without the help of the Holy Spirit, the word of God can actually become a tool used by the enemy of our souls to bring bondage instead of freedom. The devil knows the word of God better than most people! He loves to utilize Scripture for the purpose of bringing people into captivity to lies, half-truths, and deception. *Webster's Dictionary* defines a *lie* as "a statement that deviates from or perverts the truth."[146]

> If the enemy can wring the meaning out of the word of God through subtle lies and deception, then the enemy can keep people from the truth—and ultimately, from their destiny in God.

Jesus experienced the devil's attempt at misusing Scripture firsthand when he was in the wilderness for those forty days preparing for his ministry. He was tested at least three times by the devil, according to Luke 4:1-13. And, in each instance, Jesus responded to the devil with "It is written…. " Jesus was prompted by the Holy Spirit to give a response based on the written word of God. Utilizing the word of God in this way turned out to be a sword that cut right through the devil's schemes.

What is interesting in the devil's final attempt to deceive Jesus, in Luke 4:9-12, is that the devil quoted Scripture to Jesus. In this temptation, the devil attempted to have Jesus circumvent the purpose for his life by jumping from the highest point of the temple. In his attempt to deceive Jesus, the devil quoted Psalm 91:11-12. Fortunately, Jesus understood that when these verses were quoted from the lips of his adversary, they were twisted out of context and terribly misconstrued. This is why Jesus later said about the devil, "When he lies, he speaks his native language, for he is a liar and the father of lies."[147]

In this chapter, it will become clear how for many years the devil has been twisting God's word out of context regarding six verses misappropriated to gay and lesbian people. The power of this lie has unfortunately kept homosexuals, their families, and their Churches in deep bondage and pain. If the enemy can wring the meaning out of the word of God through subtle lies and deception, then the enemy can keep people from the truth—and ultimately, from their destiny in God. This is exactly what has occurred for many gays and lesbians as they have turned to the word of God for answers. Instead of discovering life in the word and a light for their path, they have found confusion and darkness. This is unfortunately true because certain passages of Scripture have been misunderstood, at times mistranslated, and even misinterpreted in such a way as to serve to *clobber* homosexuals.

Let's take a look in this chapter and in Chapter 9 at the passages of Scripture which have been coined the *clobber passages*. These Scriptures have historically been used to condemn modern-day eunuchs or gays and lesbians. They are Genesis 19, Leviticus 18:22 and 20:13, Romans 1:24-26, 1 Corinthians 6:9, and 1 Timothy 1:10.

## Genesis 19

Most Christians have heard it taught that Sodom and Gomorrah and the surrounding cities were destroyed by God because of the sin of homosexuality. If this is what you have been taught, you probably associate the term *sodomite* to a male homosexual. This is unfortunate because the meaning of "sodomite" is connected to cultic religious practices. According to *Unger's Bible Dictionary,* this term is not related to the inhabitants of Sodom but rather to " …the emasculated priests of Cybele," or to " …men consecrated to the unnatural vice of Sodom as a religious rite."[148] It's amazing what a little truth can do to bring light on the subject.

I think it is always important, when possible, to start any study with the highest authority in the Scriptures: the words of Jesus. Apparently, Jesus had something to say about the cities of Sodom and Gomorrah. He told his disciples when he sent them out to minister that the cities not welcoming of them would be worse off than Sodom and Gomorrah. Here are Jesus' words as recorded in Matthew 10:14-15:

"If anyone will not welcome you or listen to your words, shake the dust off your feet when you leave that home or town. I tell you the truth, it will be more bearable for Sodom and Gomorrah on the day of judgment than for that town."

Jesus gave these instructions to his apostles and then later he gave the same instructions to the seventy disciples who were sent out to evangelize.[149] In both of these instances, Jesus makes clear that the "sin of Sodom" was their inhospitality. There is never a reference by Jesus to sexual immorality and certainly not to homosexuality in regard to Sodom and Gomorrah. What we will discover is that sexual immorality was not the most important sin of these ancient people. Instead, Jesus made clear that the grossest sin of these ancient cities was related to inhospitality. These cities were finally rejected by God because they specifically rejected God's messengers and subsequently, God's message. Jesus made it clear that it would be possible for others to be judged similarly if they too were inhospitable to the ones God sent to them.

Now, let's take a look at the story's original telling, which is in Genesis 19. In Genesis 19, we have two angels who arrive in Sodom in order to ascertain if the city is as ungodly as the outcry from heaven. Lot, the nephew of Abraham, greets the two men at the gates of the city and invites the two angels, who appear to be men, to share in the hospitality of his home. Since hospitality is the main factor in this story, at least according to Jesus, let's take a moment and talk about its importance in ancient culture.

The law of hospitality is virtually lost in our culture today, yet it was central to the people of the ancient near east. Life in these cultures depended upon mutual honor, which became the basis for the law of hospitality. When strangers would enter a city, it was expected that whoever first met the strangers would offer them the help that they needed. Usually this meant access to water, food, and shelter for a period of time. What was at stake was the survival of the strangers to some degree. Imagine traveling through a desert land where there is no hotel, motel, or fast food restaurant awaiting your arrival. Your survival would be dependent on others welcoming you and giving you necessary provisions. The law of hospitality dictated that the visitors would be protected from any harm, even at the cost of the life of the one who offered the hospitality.

Now, let's see how the law of hospitality is violated in the story of Sodom and Gomorrah. Lot, who is considered righteous, opens up his home for the two men. In contrast, all the other city residents are opposed to this hospitality provided by Lot and they seem intent on wickedness. Genesis 19:4-5 gives us a good description of the people of Sodom seeking out the two men.

> "But before they lay down, the men of the city, even the men of Sodom, compassed the house round, both old and young, all the people from every quarter: And they called unto Lot, and said unto him; Where are the men which came in to thee this night? Bring them out unto us, that we may know them." (KJV)

First of all, let me clarify that it is incorrectly believed that only the men of Sodom surrounded Lot's house. It is also taught by many Christians that the whole city of Sodom was inhabited by only homosexual males. This is foolishness. It would be very difficult for a city, or any civilization for that matter, to exist made up of just homosexuals. Surely Lot's daughters were not married to homosexual males. In this passage of Scripture, the Bible makes clear that both men and women surrounded Lot's house. The word translated into English in verse 4 as *men* actually means *mortals* and is better translated as people. The passage goes on to say that people, both old and young, and then *all the people from every quarter* came and surrounded Lot's house.

Another issue that is important is that these people who surrounded Lot's house indicate that they want to *know* the two men. This Hebrew word, *yada*[150] is used 943 times in the Hebrew text and in only ten instances does it have a sexual connotation. Nevertheless, we can see as this story plays out that these men and women are intent on harming the two visitors and this seems to include sexual abuse.

81

The story continues in Genesis 19:6-8:

> "And Lot went out at the door unto them, and shut the door after him, And said, I pray you, brethren, do not so wickedly. Behold now, I have two daughters which have not known man; let me, I pray you, bring them out unto you, and do ye to them as is good in your eyes: only unto these men do nothing; for therefore came they under the shadow of my roof." (KJV)

Lot's words and actions only confirm the fact that the crowd's desire is to physically and sexually harm the visitors. Why else would Lot offer his two daughters to the crowd, and confirm that they are virgins, unless Lot understood that they wanted to harm his guests in some sexual way? Now, the offering by Lot of his two daughters to be abused by the crowd is despicable to us today. We wonder how any father could even consider placing a family member in danger, much less consider placing two young women in the hands of a mob. It is unbelievable to us today, but nevertheless true, that two strong cultural factors led Lot to do this very thing.

First of all, we have already discussed the importance of the law of hospitality during this time. What we have to try to understand is that the well-being of these two men is now in the hands of Lot and he is required by this law to even offer himself if necessary in order to save the men from any harm. This seems contrary to our Western ways, but this type of hospitality still exists in certain areas of the world today.

Secondly, the position of women in the ancient world is hard for us to understand today. Yet, the Bible is set in culture and so we get the good, the bad, and the ugly when we look at the history of humanity. What is interesting, however, is that the Bible also gives us God's verdict on many of these ancient cultural ways because God is a redeeming God. In this story, what we do know is that the life of a female was not as valuable as the life of a male. Males had a superior position to that of women. This superior position was not a part of God's original plan for humanity. God created male and female equal. However, when sin entered the world, then relationships became twisted and distorted. The inferior position of women began in the first family in Eden when God said to the woman, " …and he will rule over you" (Gen. 3:16b).

Part of the curse of sin has been the fact that males began to rule over women and the position of women became one of subordination to men. What is wonderful is that God did something really wonderful for women in this same garden. God spoke to the serpent and said he would be crushed by the Messiah who would come through the "woman." What is interesting about this promise, known as the protevangelium in Genesis 3:15, is that normally descendants were always spoken as coming from the male. But, in this instance, I believe that God was highlighting and foreshadowing that the role of women and the position of women would be restored through Jesus' death on the cross. The New Testament confirms this very thing when it says in Galatians 3:13, that "Christ redeemed us from the curse of the law by becoming a curse for us…. " For us today, all we can do is be thankful that God has taken care of this injustice through Christ and then begin to live it out.

Now, to fast forward through the remainder of the Sodom and Gomorrah story, it is the two angels who intervene in the situation. They cause blindness to come upon the crowd and then rescue Lot

There is no link to homosexuality per se in this story but the Biblical account does seem to infer that rape of the male visitors was intended."

and his family. Most of you remember that Lot's wife looked back. Apparently she perished and became a pillar of salt when the cities were destroyed by fire. Only Lot and his two daughters end up being saved from the fire and brimstone that fell from heaven upon Sodom and Gomorrah and the surrounding cities.

So, what was the sin of Sodom? There is no doubt that the residents of the city were wicked. Their wickedness was first noted in heaven and then confirmed when the two angels visited the city. Apparently, only Lot is found to be righteous. And, there is no doubt that there was harm, both physical and sexual, intended for the visitors. There is no link to homosexuality *per se* in this story but the biblical account does seem to infer that rape of the male visitors was intended. It is important to understand that any anal rape that might have been intended as part of the abuse in this story is not really related to sexuality. Rape can be heterosexual or homosexual in nature, but it is, nevertheless, always an act of violence against another human being.

In the case of Abner Louima's assault in New York City on August 9, 1997, sexuality had nothing to do with police officers assaulting him. The officers beat him, and then when he was under arrest at the 70th Precinct station house, they held him down with his hands cuffed behind his back, and jammed a broken off plunger handle into his rectum. Same-sex orientation or homosexuality had nothing to do with this act of violence and hatred. Later, one of the officers took the broken and bloodied plunger handle and used it to break Louima's teeth. These heterosexual officers were expressing hatred through extreme violence which included sodomizing this young, Haitian immigrant. Later, one officer was sentenced to thirty years in prison and a second received a prison sentence of five years for crimes against this young man.[151] It is clear that sexuality has nothing to do with anal rape. Rape is simply a crime of hatred, power, and violence.

It is important to note that there is an identical story in Judges 19 to that of the Sodom and Gomorrah story in Genesis 19. This time, the sin of Sodom has come much closer to home in that this story is about the people of the tribe of Benjamin in the city of Gibeah. Like the Sodom and Gomorrah story, the people of Gibeah surround the house of an elderly man who has offered hospitality to a traveling Levite and his concubine. And, once again, the crowd asks the elderly man to bring out the Levite so that they might *know* (*yada*) him. The elderly man in this instance offers to throw out his virgin daughter as well as the Levite's concubine to the wicked people. It seems that, again, the men and women in the crowd have physical and sexual abuse on their minds.

Yet, this is where the two stories depart. For in this story there are no angels present to intervene. And, sadly enough, there is no divine intervention when the Levite sends his concubine out to the wolves, so to speak. The biblical story continues with the concubine woman being abused and raped throughout the night and then left for dead in the morning. What I find just as appalling as the rape in this story is the last moments of this woman's life. This woman crawls to the threshold of the house where no one is even watching for her or seemingly concerned. And, there she dies. It is hard for us to understand today how a woman could be willingly offered to a mob of wicked people for the purposes of abuse.

Still, the greatest departure from the Sodom and Gomorrah story is that the rape of Gibeah has never been used as condemnation of homosexuality. Interestingly enough, this biblical account has also never been used as condemnation of heterosexuality either.

## Other Scriptural references to the Sodom and Gomorrah story

In order for us to correctly understand the Genesis 19 biblical account, it is important for us to see what other biblical writers had to say about it. We have already seen that Jesus mentioned the sin of Sodom and Gomorrah as inhospitality caused by great wickedness. Jesus' words will guide us as we look at three other references to the Sodom and Gomorrah story.

First of all, let's take a look at what the prophet Ezekiel had to say about the sin of Sodom as recorded in Ezekiel 16:49-50:

> "Now this was the sin of your sister Sodom: She and her daughters were arrogant, overfed, and unconcerned; they did not help the poor and needy. They were haughty and did detestable things before me. Therefore I did away with them as you have seen."

In this list of Sodom's sins there is nothing really new to us. It isn't hard for us to imagine the people of Sodom as prideful, overfed, unconcerned, haughty, and unwilling to help the poor and needy. This seems to fit right in with Jesus' assessment of their sin as gross inhospitality.

There is one thing in the list of sins, however, that is often misunderstood as a reference to homosexuality. It is that the people of Sodom did *detestable things* before God. This phrase in the King

James Version of the Bible is *committed abominations*. Some people have been taught that the worst possible sin, or what God considers an abomination, is homosexual sex. We will delve into a more thorough study of this word later on in this chapter. Suffice to say that what this phrase is conveying is idolatrous practices. The word translated into English as "abomination" or "detestable" is the Hebrew word *Toebah* which means "something disgusting, an abhorrence, especially idolatry or concretely, an idol."[152] If you check the usage of this word in the Old Testament, you will find that it is almost always connected to idolatrous worship.

It is not difficult to believe that the people of Sodom and Gomorrah had their hearts turned away from God. We know that they were wicked and that not even ten righteous people lived within the city limits. The fact that Ezekiel describes their worship as that of *committing abominations* before God is not surprising. In fact, the mention of Sodom's sins by the prophet Ezekiel is to let the people of Jerusalem know that they too have been unfaithful in their worship of God. Ezekiel even proclaims that Jerusalem's condition is worse than that of Sodom's. So, this reference to *committing abominations* which Ezekiel provides is not meant to be a condemnation of homosexuality.

Secondly, some folks have attempted to see homosexuality in two verses found in the book of Jude. Let's take a look at these two verses in Jude 6-7:

> "And the angels which kept not their first estate, but left their own habitation, God hath reserved in everlasting chains under darkness unto the judgment of the great day. Even as Sodom and Gomorrah, and the cities about them in like manner, giving themselves over to fornication, and going after strange flesh, are set forth for an example, suffering the vengeance of eternal fire." (KJV)

People have assumed that any reference to Sodom and Gomorrah like the one in Jude 7 is surely a condemnation of homosexuality. After the assumption is made, however, then they are left with having to

86

explain how fornication and going after strange flesh has anything to do with homosexuality. The reference of going after *strange flesh* is not a reference to homosexuality. It is actually a condemnation of sexual activity with angels. That is why the phrase, *in like manner* is used in Jude 7. This phrase in Jude 7 ties the mention of angels in Jude 6 to the Sodom and Gomorrah destruction. Both of these stories have angels in common.

The first reference in Jude 6 to angels "which kept not their first estate" is about the biblical account of Genesis 6:1-4. In this biblical account, angels participated in sexual intercourse with women creating a new race of people called the Nephilim. The result of this grievous sin is that God wiped out all of humanity with the exception of Noah and his family. Apparently, God really dislikes angels having sex with human beings and considers it against nature. The connection between the Genesis 6:1-4 episode alluded to in Jude is that the people of Sodom almost unknowingly entered into the same sin. This is hardly a reference to homosexuality!

Another reference to Sodom and Gomorrah that I should mention is found in 2 Peter 2:4-8. It is not necessary to go into much detail about this passage because once again a parallel is drawn between the destruction in Noah's day and that of Sodom and Gomorrah. What ties these two events together is the same sin mentioned previously of sexual activity between angels and humans.

What we have seen so far is that the Bible seems to be silent on the issue of homosexuality when it comes to the Sodom and Gomorrah story. Jesus stated what the grave issue was for Sodom and Gomorrah when he sent out his disciples. He said that these cities were judged because they did not receive the angels who were sent to them. Apparently, these angels were sent to also warn the people of their sinful ways. It is really important that we today do not reject God's messengers who are sent to bring us a message from God. If Jesus, the prophet Ezekiel, the apostle Peter, and the writer of Jude are silent about homosexuality when it comes to the Genesis 19 account, then perhaps we should be, too. It is unfortunate that after thousands of years, suddenly voices would rise up in an attempt to link homosexuality to the destruction of Sodom and Gomorrah.

## Various interpretations of the Sodom and Gomorrah Story

Now, if the biblical comments about Sodom and Gomorrah are void of any reference to homosexuality, then how did the destruction of these cities ever get linked to the condemnation of homosexuality? Interestingly enough, these misguided interpretations of the story, which are upheld by many within the Church today, came into existence at a much later date. The story was initially never seen as a condemnation of homosexuality by the Hebrew people.[153] In fact, the Talmudic references to homosexuality never refer to Genesis 19.[154] It wasn't until hundreds of years later that damaging interpretations began to surface in Jewish writings like the Pseudepigrapha, which never became part of the Hebrew canon, and the Apocrypha, which is only recognized by the Roman Catholic and Greek Orthodox Church. These Jewish writings were created from approximately 200 BC to 100 AD, ending around the time of the New Testament period. In much of these writings, when the sexual activities of the people of Sodom and Gomorrah are addressed, the Jewish writers seem to condemn excesses that are both heterosexual and homosexual in nature.[155]

Finnish Old Testament scholar Martti Nissinen provides a general overview of these Jewish writings in the following:

> Sodom is mentioned often as the quintessence of a perverted lifestyle and abandonment of God's law. For instance, in the Book of Jubilees, Sodom is frequently represented as the symbol of corruption, fornication, and idolatry (13:17, 16:5-6; 20:5; 22:22; 37:10). These writings, more than those of the Hebrew Bible, see clear sexual nuances in the sin of Sodom. Quite often there is apprehension about heterosexual recklessness. Sodom's fornication is associated with lechery with women (Test. Benj. 9:1). Adultery, prostitution, and marrying a Gentile woman are also included among the sins of Sodom and

are seen as transgressions of the Torah (Test. Levi 14:6-7).[156]

As you can see, Jewish writers began to add their own twist to the Sodom and Gomorrah biblical account. The strongest writings against homosexual sex are from the Jewish historian Flavius Josephus (37-100 AD) and the Jewish philosopher Philo of Alexandria (20 BC-50 AD) during the time of the New Testament.

As far as interpretations of Sodom and Gomorrah within Christian writings, there is little mention of homosexuality until the thirteenth century, according to historian John Boswell.[157] He explains that Christian writers such as Origen, who castrated himself in order to keep from sexual temptation, did not see homosexuality in the Sodom story. And even Saint Ambrose, who recognized a sexual nuance to the story, nevertheless saw the moral issue as one of hospitality. Another Church leader, John Cassian, likewise did not blame any homosexual nuance for Sodom's fall but rather gluttony. However, as we enter into the Middle Ages, the tolerance of homosexuality began to deteriorate as well as the biblical interpretations. It is dishonest for Christians today to join in with some voices from the Dark Ages and begin to link the destruction of Sodom and Gomorrah to homosexuality.

My admonition is to adhere to the words of Jesus and understand that God's judgment upon these ancient people of Sodom and Gomorrah was due to their inhospitality to the people sent to them. Their inhospitality was lived out in extreme disregard for the worth of others and resulted in violence and sexual domination. Ultimately, these people were condemned by God because of their rejection of God's message given by God's messengers.

I would like to address one last reference given to us by Jesus of the Sodom and Gomorrah incident. This reference

> If Jesus, the prophet Ezekiel, the apostle Peter, and the writer of Jude are silent about homosexuality when it comes to the Genesis 19 account, then perhaps we should be, too.

in Luke 17 is quite humorous in light of the fact that many Christians still today misinterpret God's destruction of Sodom and Gomorrah as support for the condemnation of homosexuality. Jesus seems to have anticipated this transition in interpretation that gave rise during his earthly ministry. Here in Luke's Gospel there is a surprising twist to Jesus' statements about Sodom and Gomorrah.

Jesus is found teaching his disciples in this passage of Scripture on how the people were unprepared for the destructions that visited them during both the time of Noah and Lot. He then likens these two incidents—the flood and the destruction of the cities of Sodom and Gomorrah—as to how it will be in his second coming. And then, with the Sodom and Gomorrah story still ringing in the ears of the people, Jesus quite intentionally makes mention of two men sleeping in the same bed together. I am sure that people's jaws dropped open as Jesus taught them.

> **Ultimately, these people were condemned by God because of their rejection of God's message given by God's messengers.**

Here is the biblical account found in Luke 17:28-30 and 34-36:

> Likewise also as it was in the days of Lot; they did eat, they drank, they bought, they sold, they planted, they builded; But the same day that Lot went out of Sodom it rained fire and brimstone from heaven, and destroyed them all. Even thus shall it be in the day when the Son of Man is revealed. ...I tell you, in that night there shall be two men in one bed; the one shall be taken, and the other shall be left. Two women shall be grinding together; the one shall be taken, and the other left. Two men shall be in the field, the one shall be taken, and the other left. (KJV)

Jesus mentions two men in one bed together quite purposefully.[158] To an audience where some would be equating God's judgment of Sodom and Gomorrah with homosexual sex acts, this statement contradicted that myth. Jesus set the record straight by equating eternal life as contingent upon the condition of the individual's heart. To Jesus, if you were his disciple, it meant that you were living a life of obedience to God. In Jesus' illustration, one man is clearly a disciple regardless of the fact that he is sleeping in the same bed with another man. What Jesus was communicating is that eternal life is not based upon sexuality, but upon having your heart prepared and ready.

## Leviticus 18:13 and 20:13

There are two almost identical verses found in Leviticus that are frequently used to condemn homosexuality. They are probably the most commonly known verses out of all six of the *clobber passages* and the most misunderstood as well.

> "You shall not lie with a male as with a woman. It is an abomination."[159] ~Leviticus 18:22 (NKJV)

> "If a man lies with a male as he lies with a woman, both of them have committed an abomination. They shall surely be put to death. Their blood shall be upon them."[160] ~Leviticus 20:13 (NKJV)

It is in studying these two verses that we are really introduced to the concept of idolatry. We will also discover what God really means by the word *abomination.*

These two verses belong to what is known as the Mosaic Law. The Law of Moses began with the Ten Commandments given by God to Moses. These Ten Commandments were written down by Moses so the people could follow them (see Exod. 20 and Deut. 5). Other laws were also given by God to Moses so that the Hebrew nation could live by them. These laws are listed in the books of Leviticus, Numbers, and Deuteronomy. In total, there are 623 laws in the Mosaic Law.

## The Law of Love

It should be noted that New Testament Christians are no longer obligated to follow these Old Testament laws. It is interesting that Christians who misunderstand Leviticus 18:22 and 20:13 as condemnations of homosexuality also err in placing Christians on this side of Jesus' cross back under the Old Covenant! If Christians today want to keep the Mosaic Law, then they should go ahead and try.

There is no doubt that these very Christians would soon discover that many of the Old Testament laws are repressive by today's standards. For example, Deuteronomy 25:5-10 commands levirate marriage, where a brother is required to marry his dead brother's wife if there is no offspring. This law seems absurd for us today. And, to make matters worse, if the dead man's brother is already married himself, then this law would conflict with the New Testament requirement that a man only have one wife. Another law that would get women upset today is found in Deuteronomy 22:28-29. This law states that if a man rapes a virgin who is not engaged to be married, he is obligated to marry her and make a monetary payment to the virgin's father. I imagine that most rape victims today would vote to repeal this particular law.

> Even though we have established that the Law of Moses is not applicable to Christians today, it is still important for the purposes of our study to understand what these two verses in Leviticus are all about.

It is much better to understand that God's plan is for Christians today to enjoy God's New Covenant, which is a better covenant. The Mosaic Law is obsolete for New Testament Christians because God has made provision for a new way of living (See Galatians and Hebrews especially). Let's take a look at how the teachings of the New Testament exclude Christians from keeping the Mosaic Law.

First of all, the Ten Commandments have now been replaced by Jesus with the Law of Love. This law was given to us by Jesus in Matthew 22:37-40.

"Jesus replied, 'Love the Lord your God with all your heart and with all your soul and with all your mind. This is the first and greatest commandment. And the second is like it: Love your neighbor as yourself. All the Law and the Prophets hang on these two commandments.'"

What Jesus did was summarize the Ten Commandments by distilling them into two commands. Then Jesus said that if we love God and love others, we are keeping the whole Law and adhering to what all of the prophets said. As New Testament Christians, we are no longer under the Law but are instead under a higher standard called the Law of Love. The Law of Moses is no longer the standard of living for Christians today.

The apostle Paul writes in Galatians 3:23-25, that Christians today are no longer under the supervision of the law.

"Before this faith came, we were held prisoners by the law, locked up until faith should be revealed. So the law was put in charge to lead us to Christ that we might be justified by faith. Now that faith has come, we are no longer under the supervision of the law."

The apostle Paul goes on to explain that if Christians today attempt to live under the Old Testament laws, then they actually nullify what Jesus Christ accomplished on the cross.

"I do not set aside the grace of God, for if righteousness could be gained through the law, Christ died for nothing!"
~Galatians 2:21

"But if you are led by the Spirit, you are not under law."
~Galatians 5:18

Instead of the Mosaic Law, Christians today now have the Holy Spirit available to lead them into loving God and others. Also, the apostle Paul makes clear in Romans 13:8-10 that it is love that is the fulfillment of the law.

> "Let no debt remain outstanding, except the continuing debt to love one another, for the one who loves their fellow person has fulfilled the law. The commandments, 'Do not commit adultery,' 'Do not murder,' 'Do not steal,' 'Do not covet,' and whatever other commandment there may be, are summed up in this one rule: 'Love your neighbor as yourself.' Love does no harm to its neighbor. Therefore, love is the fulfillment of the law."

All of these wonderful Scriptures provided for us in the New Testament clearly state that no Christian today is under the Mosaic Law. Instead, God has given Christians a much higher standard to live by. Even though we have established that the Law of Moses is not applicable to Christians today, it is still important for the purposes of our study to understand what these two verses in Leviticus are all about. They have been misunderstood throughout the years and so it is important to comprehend what God was addressing in these most famous of clobber passages.

**The context of Leviticus 18 and 20 as a clue to idolatry**

The first clue toward understanding these two select verses in question is found in the context of the chapters where they are placed. Let's begin by taking a look at the first few verses of Leviticus 18 in order to see what God is addressing in this chapter. Here is what Leviticus 18:1-5 states:

> "The Lord said to Moses, 'Speak to the Israelites and say to them: I am the Lord your God. You must not do as they do in Egypt, where you used to live, and you must not do as they do in the land of Canaan, where I am bringing you. Do not follow their practices. You must obey my laws and be careful to follow my decrees. I am

94

the Lord your God. Keep my decrees and laws, for the
one who obeys them will live by them. I am the Lord.'"

The beginning of Chapter 18 indicates that God is concerned with the
nation of Israel adopting the practices of the Egyptians and Canaanites.
The Hebrew nation had just lived for over 400 years in Egypt, and what
we will discover is that they had a lot of "Egypt" to get out of them.
And now the Hebrew nation was in the land of Canaan, and so God
instructed the people to not follow after the Canaanites either.

Now, it is important for us to be introduced to the practices of both
the Egyptians and Canaanites. The Egyptians were known to worship
a fertility god named Apis. This deity was represented by the shape of
a bull. In order to worship this deity, people would go and have sexual
relations with the priests and priestesses who served Apis. The reason
for this is that the people believed that if they had sexual relations before
this deity, then they would be blessed. This type of worship is known as
a fertility cult religion because of the belief that these pagan gods would
fertilize the land through rain showers bringing fruitfulness in crops,
animals, and in children. Then, in order to please the gods, the male
worshipers would in turn bring their *seed* to be given in cultic worship
practices. Obviously, God did not want his chosen nation to participate
in this type of worship which was first of all, idolatrous, and secondly,
considered unclean. Remember that the very first commandment God
gave to the nation was to not have any other gods before Yahweh. And,
the second commandment prohibited the making of an idol. So, idolatry
was the first and most serious violation of God's law for the Hebrew
nation.

Unfortunately, the Hebrew nation was enticed to worship the
Egyptian gods even after their exodus from Egypt. The Egyptian god,
Apis, seems to have been a particular stumbling block for the Hebrew
nation as seen in Exodus 32. While Moses is up on Mount Sinai for
forty days receiving the commandments from God, it seems that the
people revert back to their old ways. Exodus 32:17-25 describes a scene
where the Hebrew nation is engaged in the worship of a golden calf and

Moses, upon his return to the camp, sees the people running wild and out of control.

There were many Egyptian gods besides Apis, but this incident in Exodus 32 clearly shows the pull that the pagan worship practices had on the Hebrew nation. The feast that Aaron organizes for the people seems to be a cultic worship orgy because Exodus 32:6 says, " ...and the people sat down to eat and to drink, and rose up to play."

The Egyptian gods were not the only problem for the Hebrew nation. God also instructed them to not adopt the customs of the Canaanites. Chapter 18 makes reference to a god named Molech, who was worshiped in the Middle East and in both Egypt and Canaan. The reference to this deity is found in the verse directly preceding Leviticus 18:22. Here is what God had to say about Molech, according to Leviticus 18:21:

> "And thou shalt not let any of thy seed pass through the fire to Molech, neither shalt thou profane the name of thy God: I am the Lord." (KJV)

Molech is connected to Apis in that the idol is depicted as a man with a bull's head.[161] Since Molech demanded human sacrifices, it was common for parents to offer their seed or children to this deity as a way of invoking blessings upon their lives. Doesn't it seem clear that the issue of idolatry is front and center in this chapter of Leviticus?

Now, let's look at the context of Leviticus 20 in order to see how the topic of idolatry continues into this chapter. In Leviticus 20:1-5, we are introduced again to Molech but this time we are told that participants of this fertility cult are to receive the death penalty.

> And the Lord spake unto Moses, saying, Again, thou shalt say to the children of Israel, Whosoever he be of the children of Israel, or of the strangers that sojourn in Israel, that giveth any of his seed unto Molech; he shall surely be put to death: the people of the land shall stone him with stones. And I will set my face against that man, and will cut him off from among his people;

because he hath given of his seed unto Molech, to defile my sanctuary, and to profane my holy name. And if the people of the land do any ways hide their eyes from the man, when he giveth of his seed unto Molech, and kill him not: then I will set my face against that man, and against his family, and will cut him off, and all that go a whoring after him, to commit whoredom with Molech, from among their people. (KJV)

In the introduction to Leviticus 20, God is prohibiting the nation of Israel from participating in the cultic worship practices specifically related to Molech. We have already noted that worshipers of Molech would offer their seed or children to the deity as a human sacrifice. This practice was actually adopted by King Ahaz, a King of Judah, when he "sacrificed his son in the fire," according to 2 Kings 16:3. Scripture condemns this act of pagan worship by King Ahaz and states that he followed the *abominations* of the nations.

It is important to understand that the *giving of seed* unto Molech, found in Leviticus 18:21 and Leviticus 20:2-4, also signifies sexual relations. In this case, *seed* would refer to semen. Although it is true that the worship practices for the god Molech included child sacrifice, it is also true that male worshipers would enter into sexual relations with the priests and priestesses in order to offer their seed to the fertility god.

In Leviticus 20:1-5, the phrase used three times of "giving of seed" is actually the Hebrew word *zera*. The meaning of the Hebrew word *zera* is "seed, sowing. and offspring."[162] This is the same word used in Leviticus 18:21 where it says: "And thou shalt not let any of thy seed pass through [the fire] to Molech, neither shalt thy profane the name of thy God: I am the Lord." (KJV)

> You see, the word "abomination" found in both of these clobber passages is actually a key to understanding God's original intent behind the prohibitions.

Bible translators have added words to this verse making the seed pass through "the fire," which is confusing. The confusion stems from the fact that the real meaning of Leviticus 18:21 is the passing of semen in sexual relations and not child sacrifice. This is made clear in Gesenius's Lexicon, where particularly the word *seed* used in Leviticus 18:21 is compared to that of Leviticus 15:16.[163] The Leviticus 15:16 verse makes the case for the seed in Leviticus 18:21 being semen since it specifically says: "And if any man's seed of copulation go out from him, then he shall wash all his flesh in water, and be unclean until the even." (KJV) In the same way, the primary meaning in Leviticus 20:2-4 of the phrase "giving of seed," is also the passing of semen through sexual relations.

Through this study of the Hebrew word *zera* we can see that Leviticus 18:21 is specifically prohibiting cultic sexual relations. The very next verse, Leviticus 18:22, is also prohibiting sexual relations associated with cultic worship. It is helpful to read Leviticus 18:21 and Leviticus 18:22 together in order to see how they both relate to cultic sexual acts in the worship of Molech. Here is Leviticus 18:21 and 22 together:

"And thou shalt not let any of thy seed pass through [the fire] to Molech, neither shalt thou profane the name of thy God: I am the Lord. Thou shalt not lie with mankind, as with womankind: it is abomination." (KJV)

I see Leviticus 18:21 as a specific prohibition of passing male semen as a sacrifice to the god Molech while Leviticus 18:22 prohibits specifically the anal sex involved in a male passing his seed to another male as a sacrifice to Molech. In the one case, God disliked the Israelite men passing their semen as a sacrifice to a pagan god. In the other, God disliked the Israelite men lying with other males as with a woman in idolatrous fashion. What is clear about both references is that they are descriptions of cultic worship practices.

Since the word "abomination" is in each of these two clobber passages, it is absolutely plain that God is prohibiting a specific sexual behavior associated with a fertility cult religion.

L. Robert Arthur, a linguist and biblical scholar, notes the following about the male to male sex acts related to the worship of Molech:

> Because each time the mention of male-male sexual activity is mentioned, it is connected with the description of its being an idolatrous practice, we must understand the proscription as being against fertility cult worship activity. Molech is intimately connected with the Egyptian god Apis, the bull, a symbol of sexual virility. We see how this was a strong attraction to the Israelites, even in the desert. When Moses was gone too long on Mount Sinai, Aaron made the golden calf, and they began their sexual acts of worship (Exod. 32:6). So now that they were among Molech worshippers, God reinforced the prohibition against fertility cult kinds of worship with all the sexual prohibitions of Leviticus 18-20.[164]

**The word "abomination" as a clue to idolatry**

Another significant factor in the Leviticus 18:22 and 20:13 verses is that they both share the word "abomination." Many Christians have taken this as ammunition that all male to male sexual relations are therefore condemned by God as abominations. Yet, when God gave these two laws to the Hebrew nation, the laws were understood in the context of what the word meant in that culture. You see, the word "abomination" found in both of these clobber passages is actually a key to understanding God's original intent behind the prohibitions.

This word is not found in any of the other verses with specific prohibitions. In Leviticus 18 and 20, there are various sexual relations that are prohibited, but they are considered *wickedness* and not described as an "abomination." It is only in the case of a male *lying with a male as with a woman* that God specifically describes this act as an abomination. I believe that this is the case because God didn't want us to miss the point!

The word "abomination" that God included in both of these verses is the Hebrew word *to`ebah* which means "disgusting, an abhorrence;

especially idolatry or concretely an idol: abominable custom, or thing, an abomination."[165] This Hebrew word has a primary meaning associated with idolatry or concretely of an idol itself.

Since the word "abomination" is in each of these two clobber passages, it is absolutely plain that God is prohibiting a specific sexual behavior associated with a fertility cult religion. In support of this is the fact that no other law in the Law of Moses mentions male-to-male sexual relations. This silence in the law regarding male-to-male sexual relations is countered by the two prohibitions found in Leviticus 18:22 and 20:13, which squarely places the context of the two prohibitions as cultic.[166]

When the Hebrew word *to`ebah* is used in the Hebrew Scriptures, it is almost always referring to an idol or to idolatry. Let's look at some examples of where the word *to`ebah* is found elsewhere in the Scriptures to confirm its meaning. Let's begin with Deuteronomy 7:25-26, where God is concerned with the Hebrew nation being ensnared by these pagan gods.

> "The images of their gods you are to burn in the fire. Do
> not covet the silver and gold on them, and do not take
> it for yourselves, or you will be ensnared by it, for it is
> detestable [to`ebah] to the Lord your God. Do not bring a
> detestable thing [to`ebah] into your house or you, like it,
> will be set apart for destruction. Utterly abhor and detest
> it, for it is set apart for destruction."[167]

In these verses God instructs the Hebrew people to burn any idols they come across from their neighbors. These idols are clearly called *to`ebah,* or detestable things.

Another reference to *to`ebah* is found in Jeremiah 2:7 and 11 where the prophet points out to the Hebrew nation two very serious infractions.

> "I brought you into a fertile land to eat its fruit and rich
> produce. But you came and defiled my land and made
> my inheritance detestable [to`ebah]... Has a nation ever

changed its gods? (Yet they are not gods at all.) But my people have exchanged their Glory for worthless idols."[168]

Jeremiah states that the idolatrous practices of the people have actually defiled the land given to them by God and defiled the people. Literally, God's chosen people are called *to'ebah,* or detestable in this case. And, then in verse 11, Jeremiah states that what the people have done is exchange God's glory for these false gods. It is a sad state of affairs. Later, we will see that the apostle Paul speaks of this very exchange in Romans 1:23.

Unfortunately, the Hebrew nation seems to have adopted the idolatrous practices of the surrounding nations quite thoroughly, because the last prophetic voice of the Old Testament denounces this very thing in Malachi 2:11.

> "Judah has broken faith. A detestable thing [to'ebah] has been committed in Israel and in Jerusalem: Judah has desecrated the sanctuary the Lord loves, by marrying the daughter of a foreign god."[169]

After examining the word *to'ebah* in these various Scriptures, it is apparent that God really hates it! God considers it an abomination for God's people to worship anything other than him. It is a direct violation to the Ten Commandments and the Law of Love that Jesus gave to New Testament believers. We have seen that the word *to'ebah* can refer to an idol, the worship of false gods, and even to the people themselves who participate in the false worship. It is possible to say for certain that the abominable sin, therefore, is idolatry.

John Boswell confirms this fact in his explanation of the word *abomination* in his book entitled, *Christianity, Social Tolerance and Homosexuality.*

> The Hebrew word "toevah", here translated "abomination," does not usually signify something

intrinsically evil, like rape or theft (discussed elsewhere in Leviticus), but something which is ritually unclean for Jews, like eating pork or engaging in intercourse during menstruation, both of which are prohibited in these same chapters. It is used throughout the Old Testament to designate those Jewish sins which involve ethnic contamination or idolatry and very frequently occurs as part of the stock phrase "toevah ha-goyim," "the uncleanness of the Gentiles" (e.g. 2 Kings 16:3). ...Often "toevah" specifically means "idol," and its connection with idolatry is patent even within the context of the passages regarding homosexual acts.[170]

So far it is apparent that everything points toward the fact that the abominable sin is idolatry. Since the word *abomination* is used in Leviticus 18:22 and 20:13, we know that the sexual practice described is cultic. The context of Leviticus 18 and 20 only confirms the cultic nature of the prohibitions listed.

The importance of this cannot be overstated: There is, therefore, *no prohibition* in the Old Testament Scriptures against male-to-male sexual relations in general. What we have seen so far is condemnations of *cultic* male to male sexual relations solely.

It is imperative to note that the male-to-male sex in Leviticus 18:22 and 20:13 is not described through the euphemism of "uncovering the nakedness," as are all the other sexual relations. Obviously, God wanted to make sure that there was no confusion in regard to these two verses. The fact that the particular sexual relations in these two prohibitions are described as *to`ebah*, differentiates them from all the other more general sexual relations listed in Leviticus 18 and 20.

As we covered earlier, the laws listed in Leviticus 18:22 and 20:13 are not applicable to New Testament Christians. Yet, it makes one wonder why it is that out of all of the illicit sexual relations connected with these fertility cults, the "lying with a male as with a woman" is set apart. These two identical prohibitions are the only ones *specifically* considered an abomination or idolatry. One has to ask why this is the case.

I would like to put the puzzle together for us regarding these two prohibitions because they are important for us in looking next at the apostle Paul's comments in the New Testament which have been used as *clobber* passages.

### "As with a woman"

The answer to this question is found in how male-to-male sexual relations involved pagan male priests and prostitutes. We have already discussed in Chapter 3 how the priests of Yahweh were differentiated from the pagan priests by terminology. The Hebrew word for Yahweh's priests is *qadash* and it means set apart or holy.[171] In the Old Testament, God instituted priests who were set apart to draw near to God and represent God before the people. These priests were called of God to handle the holy things. The High Priest was even to come into the Holy of Holies once a year to offer a sacrifice before the Lord for the people.

In contrast to this, the Old Testament had another term for priests in *qadesh*. This term clearly designated the priest as one who served a pagan deity. *Qadesh* refers to "a (quasi) sacred person, a (male) devotee (by prostitution) to licentious idolatry; sodomite, unclean."[172] Now, just as the *qadash* were called to represent Yahweh God before the people, in like manner, the *qadesh* represented the pagan god that they were devoted to. All of these pagan gods and goddesses revealed perverted characters and natures. They were not loving or good in character, and they would demand terrible things such as child sacrifices, bestiality, orgiastic rituals, and of course, sexual relations with priests and priestesses.

> When a priest became a eunuch and donned female attire, he would be completely identified with the goddess or god.

The Hebrew Scriptures inform us that the Hebrew people did participate in the fertility cult religions with these cultic priests. Some translations of the Bible identify the *qadesh* as male shrine prostitutes instead of priests. In fact, these cultic priests or male prostitutes were expelled from the land of Israel at various times and they were even removed from the temple in a couple of instances. Here are three references to the *qadesh* found in 1 Kings 15:12, 1 Kings 22:46, and 2 Kings 23:7.

> "He [Asa] expelled the male shrine prostitutes [qadesh] from the land and got rid of all the idols his fathers had made."[173] ~1 Kings 15:12

> "He [Jehoshaphat] expelled the male shrine prostitutes [qadesh] who remained there even after the reign of his father Asa."[174] ~1 Kings 22:46

> "He [Josiah] also tore down the quarters of the male shrine prostitutes [qadesh], which were in the temple of the Lord and where women did weaving for Asherah."[175] ~2 Kings 23:7

There was a significant characteristic that marked the priests who served the deities in these fertility cult religions. The one difference between the male priests and the female priestesses is that, for the most part, the priests would undergo a gender transformation. They would become like "a woman."

I want to interject, before we get any further in this discussion on ancient pagan priests becoming "as a woman," that I do not see this process of gender transformation as related to the gender transformations of those who identify as crossdressers, transgenderists, or transsexuals. The key ingredient that marked these pagan practices was that of dedication to a pagan god or goddess. In other words, the transformations took place as part of a religious practice. What is taking place today is a process where

What is clear is that the cultic priests would become as a woman. They would adopt female attire and would usually become eunuchs as part of their service to the pagan deity.

individuals undergo various levels of gender or dress transformation in order to adjust to their true identity. This study in no way should be construed as presenting a negative view on any part of the broad range of expression that exists in sexuality and gender identity.

The most common method for this process of becoming like a woman was for a male priest or prostitute to become a eunuch. Both male priests and male prostitutes would dress like women and develop feminine physical characteristics through castration.

In his book entitled, *The Sacred Fire: The Story of Sex in Religion,* B. Z. Goldberg describes the cultic worship experience and the eunuch priests associated with Molech, also referred to as Moloch.

> As the sun was setting, the worshippers left their homes and wives, and, loaded with sacrifices, they betook themselves to the warm abode of their god. While they were on their way, a huge fire was being prepared in the pit of the furnace, and as they entered the temple, flames reflected through the bronze figure of the divinity. Cold, cruel, and metallic Moloch had become incandescent, aflame with the fire of life. …When the signal was given, the eunuch priests of Moloch marched into the temple and about the radiant figure. They came to serve this cruel, relentless god, as the priestesses paid homage to a goddess more loving and generous. While the fair sex was excluded, sexual passion persisted and seemed all the more fired because of the absence of women; and beautiful, beardless young men, their bodies soft and fragrant from the use of oils and perfumes, sold themselves to the adorers of their god, depositing on the altar of the idol the money thus earned. Within the temple, too, there were dogs trained for the same purpose and the coins received from the rental or sale of these animals, called the "price of a dog," went to the priests of Moloch. The eunuch priests constituted a caste or sect with their own rites of initiation. These were held

at night in the depths of the forest. There, in the heat of frenzy and stirred by wild music, they gashed their own bodies and ran about with blood streaming from their wounds, falling over each other as they did so.[176]

In this description of the pagan worship practices for Molech a male worshiper would deposit his seed by having anal sexual relations with a eunuch priest or male prostitute. These males in the service of Molech were beautiful and beardless. Goldberg also relates how worshipers would have intercourse with dogs as a way of depositing their seed. These descriptions of the worship of Molech help us to understand what God had in mind in giving two identical prohibitions in Leviticus 18:22 and 20:13, which state that a male lying with a male *as with a woman* is idolatrous.

Priests would castrate themselves in order to dedicate themselves to the god or goddess they desired to serve. And in so doing, these male priests would represent the deity and supposedly even take on the powers of the deity. When a priest became a eunuch and donned female attire, he would be completely identified with the goddess or god.[177]

The Babylonians and Assyrians called their male transvestite eunuch temple priests associated with the goddess Ishtar *assinu* and *kurgarru*.[178] They were known to dance, play musical instruments, wear masks, and were considered effeminate. Apparently, the goddess Ishtar had the power to turn males into women. These eunuch priests were often depicted carrying a spindle for weaving, which is a symbol of women's work.

The goddess Ishtar was also worshipped by the Canaanites as Asherah. It is interesting that 2 Kings 23:7 refers to King Josiah as removing the quarters for the *qadesh* at the temple which is where women did their weaving for Asherah. It is possible that some of the *women* were actually male transvestite eunuch priests. The fact that these priests were castrated is verified by how they were referred to as "neither male nor female," "incomplete," and "half-men." Like the priests of Molech, the *assinu* and *kurgarru* served as the receptive sexual partner of male worshipers in anal intercourse.

What is clear is that the cultic priests would become *as a woman*. They would adopt female attire and would usually become eunuchs as part of their service to the pagan deity. On the other hand, priestesses would for the most part retain their female attire even though in a few cults female worshipers would wear male attire. More importantly, it was not the custom for priestesses to mutilate their bodies in an attempt to become male.

Old Testament biblical scholar, Martti Nissinen, notes the gender transformation of the cultic priests in the following:

> In Deuteronomy there are a few gender-related commandments that can readily be seen against the background of ancient Near Eastern worship, notably those in which eunuchs are excluded from the people of Yahweh (Deut. 23:2; Isa. 56:3-5) and the prohibition of cross-dressing (Deut. 22:5). ...In postexilic Israel, at the latest, one of the distinctive features of the people of Yahweh that separated them from others seems to have been that there was no compromise of gender identification: a "third gender" role comparable to that of the Mesopotamian or Syrian devotees of the goddesses was an impossible option for an Israelite. Both castration and cross-dressing were signs of devotion to an alien deity, special traits of gender identification and gender roles that were associated with cultures forbidden to the Israelites. Mixing gender roles was not a matter of personal preference or orientation but a cultural signifier.[179]

Therefore, the male cultic priest was usually marked by castration and the wearing of female attire. Also, the type of sex offered by these male cultic priests was by and large as the receptive partner in anal intercourse. Most of the worshipers in these cults would have been male, especially since fertility cult religions emphasized the offering of seed or semen. All of these facts help us understand that the Leviticus 18:22

and 20:13 verses are describing sexual relations with cultic priests. The two identical prohibitions of a male *lying with a male as with a woman* are, in fact, proscriptions against Hebrew men engaging in cultic sexual acts as worship with cultic priests.

Notice that the two prohibitions are directed to the Hebrew men and not to the cultic priests. At the time, these cultic religions were considered Gentile religions. It was assumed that there would be no Hebrew males who would become cultic priests and especially go through the initiation of castration. We mentioned this in Chapter 3, but Deuteronomy 23:17-18 stipulates that no Israelite man or woman is to become a cultic priest or priestess.

> However, the most important factor behind God's abhorrence of this particular form of cultic sexual activity was that in engaging in sexual relations with the cultic priests, the Hebrew men were in fact joining themselves to the pagan god or goddess.

We have identified the two parties in the sexual liaison described as a *male lying with a male as with a woman.* First of all, the prohibitions given by God are directed toward the Hebrew men in the nation of Israel. Secondly, we have seen that the cultic priests fit the description of a male who is *as a woman.* They were usually eunuch or transvestite priests who were the receptive partner in anal intercourse.

It is interesting to note that all of the sexual relations listed in Leviticus 18 and 20 are addressed to Hebrew men. Also, the sexual relations being prohibited are all described through relationships. For example, Leviticus 18:7 prohibits a Hebrew male from uncovering the nakedness of his father's wife or his mother. The only two verses where a relationship is not indicated is, in fact, the Leviticus 18:22 and 20:13 verses. In the description of a male *lying with a male as with a woman,* we can see that the verses are not depicting a next of kin or a relative of the Hebrew male. The Hebrew men would not have been related to the cultic priests generally because the priests would have been Gentiles. This is just further corroboration that the description of *lying with a male as with a woman* is a prohibition for sexual relations with cultic priests.

A final observation is that the laws in Leviticus 18:22 and 20:13 seem to only prohibit men from having sexual relations with cultic priests. It makes one wonder why there is no similar prohibition against Hebrew men having sexual relations with cultic priestesses. I believe that the reason why the priestesses are not even addressed is because women in the Hebrew culture were mostly subservient to men. The men had the authority and power in relationships while women were always to be under the care of a male, even as the possession of a male. This perspective originated in the curse of the wife being ruled by the husband described in Genesis 3:16. A second reason why cultic priestesses are not mentioned in these two laws is because the *qadesh* were juxtaposed to the *qadash*. There were no female priestesses in service of Yahweh God, but only male priests.

Furthermore, the penis was considered the symbol of strength and power for the male in the ancient east. Vows were made and covenants sealed by the placing of the hand of the one party on the *thigh* or penis of the other. This is seen in Genesis 24:2-3 when Abraham placed his servant's hand under his thigh and then had him swear to obtain a wife for Isaac from Abraham's relatives. It is interesting that in castration it is this very symbol of power and strength that is offered by a pagan priest to the god or goddess. The offering of one's member in this way was to seal the covenant with the deity. It was an irrevocable offering!

It is reminiscent of how God instituted circumcision for all of the males who were in the Hebrew nation beginning with Abraham. The act of circumcision was a sign of the covenant established between the Hebrew male and God. In essence, what it symbolized was the male's power and strength being "cut back" as an act of submission to God as Lord. In the New Testament, because the curse of the husband ruling over the wife is broken in Christ Jesus, spiritual circumcision becomes a requirement for both male and female believers. For the first time since the Garden of Eden, mutual submission is the key.

Therefore, I see that the key to the prohibitions in Leviticus 18:22 and 20:13 is in the identification of cultic priests as males who presented themselves *as a woman*. God only considered Hebrew males *lying with a male as with a woman* as an abomination. All the other sexual relations listed are considered wickedness or perversion. But, in God's eyes there was something intrinsically idolatrous and abhorrent about the Hebrew males engaging in cultic worship with these cultic priests.

There are several reasons for this distinction. First, the Mosaic Law already dictated God's dislike of emasculation as seen in Deuteronomy 23:1. No one who was emasculated could participate in the worship of Yahweh. Perhaps this is because of the development of man-made eunuchs. Also, the fact that the cultic priests offered this particular member of their body to the deity as a seal of their covenant made the covenant irrevocable in a way.

However, the most important factor behind God's abhorrence of this particular form of cultic sexual activity was that in engaging in sexual relations with the cultic priests, the Hebrew men were in fact joining themselves to the pagan god or goddess. This is what made this particular type of cultic sexual relations so abhorred and distinct. The anal sex was not distinct. Rather, what was distinct is that in joining themselves to the cultic priests a spiritual transference took place. It was as if they were uniting with the god or goddess which made the sexual union especially idolatrous.

Author David F. Greenberg speaks of this very union in regards to the priests and priestesses of the goddess, Ishtar.

> Although Ishtar was the goddess of love and had many lovers, she was childless. The female hierodules who consecrated themselves to her were called *naditu*, barren, because their sexual practices could not result in pregnancy. It was in imitation of the goddess and her divine partners that they and their male counterparts in the priesthood submitted to anal sex. The male worshipers who had intercourse with the priests and priestesses were uniting with the goddess herself.[180]

Likewise, when the Hebrew men participated in sexual relations with the priests of Molech, they were uniting with Molech. This is the reason why this particular cultic sexual activity was viewed by God as distinctly idolatrous. Remember that Molech is specifically referred to in Leviticus 18:21, immediately preceding Leviticus 18:22. Molech is also referred to in the beginning of Leviticus 20, before verse 13 prohibits Hebrew males lying with a male as with a woman. The abominable sin is idolatry; the abominable sexual act is uniting with the pagan deity through relations with a cultic priest.

In light of this, you can see that it is dishonest to attempt to interpret Leviticus 18:22 and Leviticus 20:13 as condemnations of homosexuality. First of all, Christians today, regardless of their sexuality, are not under the supervision of the Law. More importantly, it is apparent that these two laws in the Holiness Code are misappropriated when they are applied to gay and lesbian people today. This is especially true when the homosexuals are Christians and living a life of love according to the Law of love. Two Christian gay men engaging in loving intimacy as part of their covenant together has nothing to do with *lying with a male as with a woman*. They are not idolatrous. They are not acting in lust. And they are not uniting with a pagan god or goddess.

# 9

# CRACKING THE CODE

"But when he, the Spirit of truth, comes, he will guide
you into all truth." ~John 16:13

When I first started to pastor, I noticed that many of the gay and
lesbian Christians who came to Church did not bring their
Bibles. It was only after much teaching of God's word and being in an
atmosphere of freedom through the Holy Spirit that they endeavored to
find comfort once again from the Bible. Although it usually took some
time, it was always a joy to see these precious believers begin to bring
their Bibles to worship services.

We are told that when Jesus appeared to his disciples after his death
and resurrection, "He opened their minds so they could understand the
Scriptures."[181] I'm sure Jesus had to explain much from the Hebrew
Scriptures to his disciples so they could understand that he was the
Messiah and that his death and resurrection had been foretold. Jesus

had to teach his disciples how to apply the Scriptures to their present lives and conditions. Today we have to allow the Holy Spirit to open up our minds and teach us correct application of God's word. The Holy Spirit knows the code that will open the safe, so to speak, and allow the treasure of God's word to be opened up to us properly.

This chapter is dedicated to the three New Testament *clobber passages*. The truth of Romans 1:24-27, 1 Corinthians 6:9, and 1 Timothy 1:10 must be opened up to us by using the correct code or combination. The cultural context and, specifically, the cultic religious practices of the ancient world must be considered so that you can crack the code of these wonderful New Testament Scriptures. Now that we have become very familiar with the fertility cult practices of the ancient East from the previous chapter, we have the code that will allow us to open up these Scriptures fully and comprehend what the Holy Spirit is saying to us through them.

The cultural context and, specifically, the cultic religious practices of the ancient world must be considered so that you can crack the code of these wonderful New Testament Scriptures.

## The apostle Paul and cultic worship practices

It is significant that the apostle Paul is the author of these three New Testament *clobber passages* because we will find that he was concerned about idolatry. The very thing that was condemned in Leviticus 18:22 and 20:13 is also condemned by God on this side of the cross. Apparently, God really does not like idolatrous worship on either side of the cross.

The apostle Paul was blessed to write much of the New Testament. Inspired by the Holy Spirit after repenting from his violent persecution of Christians, Paul was a perfect candidate to write these epistles. He had personal knowledge of the great Gentile cities that he traveled to, and extensive knowledge of the Hebrew Scriptures from his background as a Jewish religious teacher.

Paul was the greatest missionary of his day. He made three missionary journeys throughout the known world at that time. Later, when Paul was arrested, he spent his remaining days in the city of Rome. Paul had first-hand knowledge of the cities in the Roman Empire. While in the city of Corinth, Paul wrote to the Church in Rome. Also, Paul spent quite a length of time in Ephesus, where he penned the letter to the Church in Corinth and also wrote to his spiritual son, Timothy.

We already discussed in chapter 4 how the city of Ephesus was known historically as a marketplace for the trade of eunuchs according to the Greek historian, Herodotus, who lived in the fifth century BC. This is the very city where Paul enjoyed great ministry for a few years and also where Timothy eventually was called to pastor. There is no doubt that Paul's familiarity with the pagan religious practices of the people in Ephesus, Corinth, Rome, and all the other cities he visited in the Roman Empire is revealed in his writings.

> This is because Paul was able to apply God's condemnation of idolatry in Israel's history to the same cultic religious practices which existed in Paul's time.

The apostle Paul was also a trained scholar in Judaism. He studied under the best teacher available to any Jewish student. According to Acts 22:3, Paul learned at the feet of Gamaliel. The status of Gamaliel is indicated in Acts 5:34, which says Gamaliel was a teacher of the law and honored by all the people. The training Paul received under his instructor Gamaliel was the best education possible in the laws of Judaism. Paul would have been very familiar with the Law and richly versed in the history of the Hebrew people and how they had prostituted themselves to other gods.

What we will discover is that Paul referred to Leviticus 18:22 and 20:13 in both 1 Corinthians 6:9 and 1 Timothy 1:10. He also begins his remarkable theological masterpiece—the letter to the Church in Rome—as a polemic against idolatry. This is because Paul was able to apply God's condemnation of idolatry in Israel's history to the same cultic religious practices which existed in Paul's time.

## 1 Corinthians 6:9 and 1 Timothy 1:10

In both 1 Corinthians 6:9 and 1 Timothy 1:10, we find two similar passages of Scripture. In these verses, Paul lists the people who will not inherit the kingdom of God because they are not adhering to sound doctrine. First Corinthians is Paul's first letter to the Church in Corinth. The letter to Timothy is also Paul's first letter that we know of to his spiritual son, Timothy, who was the pastor of the Church in Ephesus.

There are two Greek words in these Scriptures which biblical scholars have had great difficulty understanding. The first Greek word is *arsenokoitai* which is used by Paul in 1 Corinthians 6:9 and in 1 Timothy 1:10. This word is translated in the New International Version of the Bible as "homosexual offender" in 1 Corinthians 6:9 and as "pervert" in 1 Timothy 1:10. As you can see by these two translations of the same word, biblical scholars have struggled to understand the meaning of *arsenokoitai*.

The second Greek word is *malakoi* which is only used by Paul in 1 Corinthians 6:9. This word is translated in 1 Corinthians 6:9 as "male prostitute" in the New International Version of the Bible while this same word is translated as "fine" or "soft" wherever else it is found in the New Testament.

Let's examine the two lists where these two Greek words are placed in 1 Corinthians 6:9-10 and 1 Timothy 1:9-11.

"Do you not know that the wicked will not inherit the kingdom of God? Do not be deceived; Neither the sexually immoral nor idolaters nor adulterers nor male prostitutes [malakoi] nor homosexual offenders [arsenokoitai] nor thieves nor the greedy nor drunkards nor slanderers nor swindlers will inherit the kingdom of God."[182] ~1 Corinthians 6:9-10

"We also know that law is made not for the righteous but for lawbreakers and rebels, the ungodly and sinful, the unholy and irreligious; for those who kill their fathers or mothers, for murderers, for adulterers and perverts

[arsenokoitai], for slave traders and liars and perjurers—
and for whatever else is contrary to the sound doctrine
that conforms to the glorious gospel of the blessed God,
which he entrusted to me."[183] ~1 Timothy 1:9-11

## Arsenokoitai

The Greek word *arsenokoitai* is believed to be coined by the apostle
Paul.[184] This Greek word is not used elsewhere in the Bible and it is
also not found in any other literature prior to being used in Paul's
writings. *Arsenokoitai* is two Greek words
put together. The word *arsen* means man
or male and the word *koite* means bed.
Although *arsenokoitai* has baffled biblical
scholars who have translated it in various
ways, it is now believed by many scholars
to be related to the Levitical passages we
have already reviewed.

> The Greek word
> *arsenokoitai* is
> believed to be coined
> by the apostle Paul.

The Greek translation of the Old Testament is called the Septuagint.
The Septuagint would have been well-known to the whole Jewish
community and to the apostle Paul who preached in Greek during his
missionary journeys. During the third and second centuries BC, the
entire Hebrew Bible was translated into the Greek language. Therefore,
it is no surprise that the apostle Paul coined the term *arsenokoitai* as a
derivative of the Septuagint's Greek translation of Leviticus 18:22 and
20:13.

The Septuagint translates Leviticus 18:22 and 20:13 as follows[185]:

Leviticus 18:22 "kai meta *arsenos* ou koimethese *koiten*
gynaikos"

Leviticus 20:13 "kai hos an koimethe meta *arsenos*
*koiten* gynaikos… ."

Both of the above phrases are Greek translations of the phrase
"male who lies with a male as with a woman." As you can see, the two

Greek words *arsen* and *koite* are closely placed together especially in the Leviticus 20:13 verse. Therefore, it seems that the etymology of the word *arsenokoitai* is rooted in the pagan idolatrous practices referred to in Leviticus 18:22 and 20:13.

It is easy to see how the apostle Paul would have coined this word while he was preaching or teaching in Greek. It is clear that Paul is condemning the same thing in 1 Corinthians 6:9 and 1 Timothy 1:10 that the Leviticus passages condemn, namely, male worshipers lying with cultic priests as part of the fertility cult sexual practices. *Arsenokoitai* is in all likelihood referring to a male worshiper in a pagan religious cult. Paul used this word in order to tell the Greek-speaking Gentiles that if they were participating in these idolatrous practices, then they were not living according to sound doctrine nor would they inherit the kingdom of God.

Once again, these Levitical passages are condemnations of idolatrous sex acts committed by male worshipers. A *male lying with a man as with a woman* is not a reference to same-sex orientation. We already know this to be true and to be sure, it is unlikely that the vast majority of the males in the Hebrew nation were homosexual in orientation.

One has to ask if the apostle Paul encountered the same fertility cult religions during his travels that are addressed in the Holiness Code. The answer is yes. We have seen that one of the references to the word *arsenokoitai* is in Paul's epistle to the Church at Corinth. The city of Corinth was a major city in Greece not far from the city of Athens. There were two main gods worshiped in Corinth. The most popular god was the sea god, Poseidon. The city had two seaports and so people would offer sacrifices and worship the sea god in exchange for success.

A second sacred deity that was worshiped in Corinth was Aphrodite. This goddess was a goddess of love and was also referred to as Cybele, Astarte, and Ishtar. The temple of Aphrodite towered high above Corinth atop a 1,800 foot hill called the Acropolis. The temple of Aphrodite featured 1,000 female slaves who served the goddess as temple prostitutes. Immorality was considered a virtue in Corinth so much so that the verb "to corinthianize" was synonymous with "to fornicate" in the Greek of the day.[186]

Paul's usage of *arsenokoitai,* which refers to male worshipers *lying with a male as with a woman,* is understood in light of the sexual practices associated with the cult of Aphrodite. Apparently, Aphrodite was another name for Cybele, the Syrian goddess.[187] This deity was both male and female and so was depicted with a bearded face and full breasts. The cult taught that worshipers must hide their sex. Therefore, males came in female clothing and females in the clothes of males. It appeased the goddess if worshipers physically effaced their sex and it seems that hermaphrodites congregated in Aphrodite's temple in large numbers. It did not matter whether the goddess was known as Aphrodite, Cybele, Astarte, or Ishtar, because all of her worshipers engaged in erotic beatings, sadomasochism, same-sex orgies, and for the males, castration. These practices were commonplace in all of the temples dedicated to this goddess along the sea coasts where the apostle Paul traveled as a missionary.[188]

All of the mother goddesses such as Aphrodite, Cybele, Hecate, Artemis, Astarte, and others had castrated and/or transvestite priests who functioned in their temples. In the Cult of Cybele, for example, initiates mourned Cybele's androgynous lover Attis. They would re-enact his death every March, according to mythology, where in the midst of ecstatic music, they would strike themselves with sharp stones or broken pottery, and after castrating themselves, put on women's clothing.[189] Since Paul was highly educated in the Law and understood the idolatrous context of the Leviticus 18:22 and 20:13 prohibitions, it makes sense that he applied their condemnation to the same practices taking place in the cities where he traveled as a missionary. Specifically, Paul was condemning male worshipers engaging in sexual relations with cultic priests, and thereby uniting with the god or goddess.

In writing to the Church at Corinth, Paul is aware that many of the believers used to be pagans who involved themselves in these cultic practices. The very next verse after the list of vices given in 1 Corinthians 6:9-10 confirms this. The apostle Paul addresses his audience in the following:

"And that is what some of you were. But you were washed, you were sanctified, you were justified in the name of the Lord Jesus Christ and by the Spirit of our God." ~1 Corinthians 6:11

The apostle Paul then continues on in 1 Corinthians 6:13-20 to teach the Church members in Corinth that they should not engage in sexual immorality. He reminds them that their bodies are temples of the Holy Spirit and that they have been bought with a price. He also speaks to them about the uniting of themselves with a prostitute in 1 Corinthians 6:15-17:

"Do you not know that your bodies are members of Christ himself? Shall I then take the members of Christ and unite them with a prostitute? Never! Do you not know that he who unites himself with a prostitute is one with her in body? For it is said, 'The two will become one flesh.' But he who unites himself with the Lord is one with him in spirit."

It is this uniting with the prostitute that is a problem for the apostle because he understands the spiritual transference taking place when the sexual relations are cultic in nature. This is also the case when the male worshiper is sexually active with a cultic priest or prostitute as *arsenokoitai* makes reference to. In 1 Corinthians 6:16, the apostle Paul is directly speaking about a male having sexual relations with a female prostitute or "harlot" because he has just addressed a known sin in the Corinth Church in the previous chapter. The sin addressed in chapter 5 is that of a male member having sexual relations with his father's wife. If the known sin had been a male member having sexual relations with a cultic priest or male prostitute, the apostle might have elaborated on this rather than just mentioning *arsenokoitai* in 1 Corinthians 6:10.

In writing to his spiritual son, Timothy, the apostle Paul again uses the word *arsenokoitai* in a list of vices. We know that Timothy was the pastor of the Church in Ephesus, and so we must ask ourselves if Paul was addressing the same issue of cultic sexual relations when he used this word. The city of Ephesus was also where Paul spent quite a bit of time during one of his missionary journeys and where he penned 1 Corinthians. Therefore, it is an important city for us to be familiar with in order to understand the context of 1 Timothy 1:10.

Historically, the main goddess worshiped in Ephesus is "Diane of the Ephesians," as noted in Acts 19:27. Another name for Diane was Artemis. Although the goddess Diana was worshiped in thirty-three places in the known world at that time, her chief location was in Ephesus. Paul had a spiritual confrontation with this entity and many who were involved in her "magic" became believers according to Acts 19. It seems that the believers in the Church in Ephesus would have also struggled with the pull of the cultic worship practices as did some of the believers in the Church in Corinth.

> It seems that *arsenokoitai* evolved in usage from a description of the male worshiper who paid for sex with priests and male prostitutes in the temple to those who paid for sex with prostitutes outside of the cultic worship experience.

The cultic religious practices that took place in the cult of Artemis also involved castration, as described by Catherine Kroeger in "The Apostle Paul and the Greco-Roman cults of Women," found in the *Journal of the Evangelical Society*. Kroeger details how the cult of Cybele, the Syrian goddess and the cult of Artemis in Ephesus were each characterized by sex exchanges. The exchange was gruesome because males would voluntarily castrate themselves and then adopt women's garments. A relief in Rome depicts a high priest of Cybele wearing a veil, necklace, earrings, and feminine dress. In this way, the priest is considered to have exchanged his sexual identity so that he could become a she-priest.[190]

Once again, it seems that Paul's usage of the word *arsenokoitai* in the 1 Timothy 1:10 reference is related to cultic religious practices. The apostle wanted to remind the Church members that cultic worship practices and especially that of sexual liaisons with cultic priests and prostitutes were not in accord with sound Christian doctrine.

Later on, the word *arsenokotai* seems to have taken on other meanings.[191] Remember, it was the apostle Paul who coined this word. Yet, during the next two to three hundred years its usage in various non-biblical writings indicates that it evolved into a description for people who exploited others for sexual purposes. It seems that *arsenokoitai* evolved in usage from a description of the male worshiper who paid for sex with priests and male prostitutes in the temple to those who paid for sex with prostitutes outside of the cultic worship experience.

In the book entitled, *Biblical Ethics & Homosexuality*, author Dale Martin discusses the evolving meaning of *arsenokoitai* in the following:

> "I suggest that a careful analysis of the actual context of the use of *arsenokoites*, free from linguistically specious arguments from etymology or the word's separate parts, indicates that *arsenokoites* had a more specific meaning in Greco-Roman culture than homosexual penetration in general, a meaning that is now lost to us. It seems to have referred to some kind of economic exploitation by means of sex, perhaps but not necessarily homosexual sex."[192]

In other words, the term *arsenokotai* that the apostle Paul used in 1 Corinthians 6:9 and 1 Timothy 1:10 eventually came to describe the individual who would sexually exploit another, whether male or female.

Author Robin Scroggs, in *The New Testament And Homosexuality* also indicates that in 1 Timothy 1:10, Paul has placed *arsenokoitai* purposefully right in the middle between the Greek word *pornos* sometimes translated as adulterer and the Greek word *andropodistes* meaning slave trader or kidnapper.[193] It is suggested that perhaps Paul is referring to male prostitutes in *pornos*, and then males who lie with prostitutes in *arsenokoites*, and finally in dealers who procure the prostitutes in *andropodistes*. It is all very possible. Therefore, it is clear that each of the vice lists provided by Paul in 1 Corinthians 6 and 1 Timothy 1 mention people who are exploiting others or doing wrong to others.

Suffice it to say, the Greek word *arsenokoitai* should not be linked to homosexuality as it currently is in the New International Version of the Bible where *arsenokoitai* is translated as *homosexual offender*. The reason for this is because homosexuality refers to a sexual orientation rather than a sexual act. The term *arsenokoitai*—related as it is to the prohibitions of Leviticus 18:22 and 20:13—is clearly not referring to homosexuality, but rather to male worshipers in general (heterosexual or homosexual) who participated in anal sex in cultic religious practices. Later, the term came to include those who would exploit males or females sexually, and not necessarily through anal intercourse.

> It is thought that the term *malakoi* is a reference to an effeminate male prostitute or one who serves as the male receptive partner while *arsenokoitai* must refer to the males who would frequent the effeminate male prostitutes.

## Malakos

The second Greek word *malakoi* is only used by Paul in one of the clobber passages. The New International Version of the Bible has translated *malakoi* in 1 Corinthians 6:9 as "male prostitute" whereas the King James Version uses "effeminate." By the twentieth century some translators of the Bible began to link *malakoi* with *arsenokoitai* in 1 Corinthians 6:9.[194] It is thought that the term *malakoi* is a reference to an effeminate male prostitute or one who serves as the male receptive partner while *arsenokoitai* must refer to the males who would frequent the effeminate male prostitutes.

The actual word *malakoi* is found elsewhere in the New Testament and is used quite frequently in extra-biblical writings of the New Testament era. The basic meaning of *malakos* is soft or fine and in a moral sense it indicates moral weakness as in one who lacks self-control.[195] Author, John Boswell, in his book entitled, *Christianity,*

*Social Tolerance and Homosexuality* states that the term *malakos* is not associated with homosexual acts but rather has a long history of indicating masturbation.

> The word [malakos] is never used in Greek to designate gay people as a group or even in reference to homosexual acts generically, and it often occurs in writings contemporary with the Pauline epistles in reference to heterosexual persons or activity. What is more to the point, the unanimous tradition of the Church through the Reformation, and of Catholicism until well into the twentieth century, has been that this word applied to masturbation.[196]

As you can see, these various Greek terms are often times very difficult to translate into English as the meanings can change or be varied throughout Church history. I see a better translation of *malakos* as simply *effeminate*.

Martti Nissinen in *Homoeroticism In The Biblical World* states that the term *malakos* stresses femininity. He adds however that a homosexual connotation could come from effeminacy because a male who engages in a passive sexual role took on the position of a woman.[197] This understanding seems to agree with Boswell who is adamant that *malakos* is not related to homosexual orientation since heterosexual males were called this term by ancient writers.[198]

Author Dale Martin in *Biblical Ethics & Homosexuality* came to the following conclusion on the meaning of this Greek word: "*Malakia*, therefore, was a rather broad social category. It included, of course, penetrated men, but many others besides. To put it simply, all penetrated men were *malakoi,* but not all *malakoi* were penetrated men."[199] Therefore, it seems that *malakos* was at times used to refer to males who were effeminate, whether heterosexual or homosexual. And, the term apparently was also used at times to mean males who took the passive sexual role, whether heterosexual or homosexual.

With this in mind, let's look at the Greek word *malakos* as used by Jesus in his discussion centered on John the Baptist.[200] In order to understand the whole context of Jesus' statement, let's review Matthew 11:7-9.

"As John's disciples were leaving, Jesus began to speak to the crowd about John: 'What did you go out into the desert to see? A reed swayed by the wind? If not, what did you go out to see? A man dressed in fine [malakos] clothes? No, those who wear fine [malakos] clothes are in king's palaces. Then what did you go out to see? A prophet? Yes, I tell you, and more than a prophet."[201]

Here we see that Jesus used the word *malakos* twice in reference to clothing. It could be that Jesus was simply describing the clothing of those in kings' palaces as fine or soft. It is also possible that Jesus used this word in order to juxtapose John the Baptist's extreme ruggedness to the effeminacy of those in kings' palaces. After all, we know from Matthew's description of John the Baptist in Matthew 3:4, that John wore clothes made of camel's hair and had a leather belt around his waist. You could definitely say that John the Baptist was anything but effeminate.

It is certain that Jesus would have heard about Herod's three high-ranking eunuchs who were supposedly in cahoots with Herod's sons in plotting to usurp their father and take the kingship.

This discussion of John the Baptist by Jesus could also have a more concealed meaning. It is my view that Jesus was using a double-play on words when he specifically used the word *malakos* to describe the opposite characteristics of John the Baptist. In asking these three rhetorical questions, the answer is obviously a negative one until the third time. The message that Jesus is communicating here is that John the Baptist is a prophet of God. In contrast, Jesus uses the word *malakos* to describe those who are not of God.

Let's take a look at how Jesus compares John's true identity as a prophet to others whose identities evidently do not come from God. In the first rhetorical question, Jesus' description of a "reed swayed by the wind," metaphorically represents pagan priests and prostitutes. This is because historically, the fertility cults that came out of the near east were located in the desert. Also, the mention of a reed swaying in the wind could be a euphemism to effeminacy just as today effeminate men are humorously impersonated by the showing of a limp wrist.

It is interesting that 1 Kings 14:15 connects idolatry to a "reed" when it makes mention of God striking Israel "like a reed swaying in the water" because of her idolatrous behavior. Here is 1 Kings 14:15:

> "And the Lord will strike Israel, so that it will be like a reed swaying in the water. He will uproot Israel from this good land that he gave to their forefathers and scatter them beyond the River, because they provoked the Lord to anger by making Asherah poles."

Remember that the worship of the goddess Asherah by the Canaanites is linked to the cult of Ishtar. In this cult the goddess Ishtar had the power to turn males into females. The priests were male transvestite eunuch priests, taking on the powers of the goddess. In alluding to a "reed swayed by the wind," Jesus is contrasting these cultic priests to God's anointed prophet. The mention of their effeminacy in "a reed swayed by the wind" is not a condemnation of effeminacy per se, but rather a way of identifying these eunuch men who had dedicated themselves to pagan gods and goddesses.

Then, in the second rhetorical question Jesus alludes to the fact that there were others who wore *malakos* or soft clothing and they are found in kings' palaces. This is a reference to the eunuchs who served in pagan kings' palaces. There were three known eunuchs who served in King Herod's palace during Jesus' early life. It is certain that Jesus would have heard about Herod's three high-ranking eunuchs who were supposedly in cahoots with Herod's sons in plotting to usurp their father and take the kingship. The historian Josephus describes the roles of these eunuchs in his Antiquities and states that one was in charge of Herod's drink, another his food, while the third put Herod to bed.[202]

Therefore, it seems to me that the euphemism of "a reed swaying in the wind" and the word *malakos* are used by Jesus indirectly to refer to the two known roles common to man-made eunuchs. Jesus was familiar with natural-born eunuchs and man-made eunuchs, according to Matthew 19:12. Therefore, in his discussion of the authenticity of John the Baptist as a prophet of God, Jesus is contrasting John with man-made eunuchs.

In fact, what we have in 1 Corinthians 6:9 and 1 Timothy 1:10 are two Greek words which are related to cultic worship. In *arsenokoitai*, we have a reference to the male worshipers who would engage in sexual intercourse with cultic priests and prostitutes. Later this word is adopted to generally mean any male who sexually exploits a male or female person. The other term, *malakos*, seems to generally be a derogatory reference to male effeminacy and also at times to the passive male sexual role. Also, *malakos* is clearly a reference to man-made eunuchs in the service of pagan deities or royalty because of Jesus' usage of it.

Neither of these terms used in 1 Corinthians 6:9 or 1 Timothy 1:10 point to a person of same-sex orientation nor do they condemn homosexuality. In fact, *arsenokoitai* especially is related to heterosexual males who originally participated in sexual relations in fertility cults and later to males who exploited males and females sexually outside of the fertility cult aspect. The term *malakos* also cannot be used to condemn homosexuality since it refers to males who were effeminate in general and also to males who engaged in sex as the passive partner, whether heterosexual or homosexual. Then, in the words of Jesus we see that *malakos* is used indirectly to refer to those who were man-made eunuchs, which we understand to be the counterfeit of natural-born eunuchs or people of same-sex orientation.

## Romans 1:24-27

This brings us to our final *clobber passage* found in the New Testament book of Romans. This epistle to the Church in Rome is the apostle Paul's theological masterpiece regarding the grace of God. He begins the book by describing those who have rejected God's goodness and who have followed after a lie. This lie is the worship of something other than God—which is idolatry. Therefore, what we have leading up to our clobber passage in Romans 1:24-27 is Paul's polemic against idolatry.

Let's begin by looking at our final clobber passage found in Romans 1:24-27:

> Therefore, God gave them over in the sinful desires of their hearts to sexual impurity for the degrading of their bodies with one another. They exchanged the truth of God for a lie, and worshiped and served created things rather than the Creator—who is forever praised. Amen. Because of this, God gave them over to shameful lusts. Even their women exchanged natural relations for unnatural ones. In the same way the men also abandoned natural relations with women and were inflamed with lust for one another. Men committed indecent acts with other men, and received in themselves the due penalty for their perversion.

It is in Romans 1:24-27 that many Christians have found condemnation for both male and female homosexuality. This interpretation really misses the point, however, since Paul is very clearly continuing to write about idolatrous religious practices.

Not only is the apostle Paul speaking generally about idolatrous religious practices here in Romans 1, but he uses words and terms that are very specific in this regards. First of all, Paul speaks specifically in verse 22 about idols when he mentions how the people have "… exchanged the glory of the immortal God for images made to look like mortal man and birds and animals and reptiles."

Secondly, in verse 25 Paul states, "They exchanged the truth of God for a lie, and worshiped and served created things rather than the Creator…." Here, the apostle is specifically using the same language as the prophet Jeremiah who warned Israel about forsaking God for false gods. Jeremiah 2:11 says, "Has a nation ever changed its gods? (Yet they are not gods at all.) But my people have exchanged their Glory for worthless idols."

Finally, the apostle Paul uses the phrase "worshiped and served" in verse 25 which is the only time this Greek word for "worship" is used in the New Testament. This phrase in Greek usage is a reference to cultic worship.[203]

Now that it is clear that Paul has in mind idolatry, let's explore the clobber passage in Romans 1:24-27. The beginning of verse 24 starts with "Therefore" and verse 26 with "Because of this." The apostle Paul has been building a case against

> Not only is the apostle Paul speaking generally about idolatrous religious practices here in Romans 1, but he uses words and terms that are very specific in this regards.

idolatry and now he is ready to sum up the behaviors of the people who are involved in such idolatry. Once again, there is really no way of understanding what the passage in question meant to the people it was originally addressed to unless we explore the religious practices taking place in the city of Rome and the Roman Empire.

The apostle Paul wrote to the Church in Rome while he was in Corinth. We have already explored the religious practices of the people of Corinth. Paul encountered grave idolatry as he traveled in his missionary journeys to preach the Gospel to the Gentiles. Most of the cities of the ancient world would have had a patron deity or several gods that its citizens worshiped. To understand Rome, however, one must understand that it was both the seat of power and also the seat of spiritual influence.

During the time of the apostle Paul's missionary journeys, from 47-57 AD, the fertility cult religions would have been in full bloom all throughout the Gentile cities where he traveled. Paul was familiar with their practices as we have already seen in our study. Rome was known for officially adopting the first of the eastern religions, the cult of Cybele.[204] Ambassadors were sent to Asia to bring back a black meteorite that was identified as the image of the goddess. When the statue arrived in Rome, a temple for it was built on the Palatine. A prerequisite for the priesthood was emasculation. Therefore, when the worship of Cybele was first introduced in Rome, there was a disdain for the eunuch priests since the Romans hated emasculation. Yet, even after forbidding their citizens from being initiated as priests, the practice still became widespread. Later the Church historian, Eusebius, Bishop of Caesarea (AD 260–340), wrote that these priests were still operating in this type of worship during his time.[205]

In light of these practices, Paul mentions in Romans 1:27 a curious thing in regards to men. He states that they "… received in themselves the due penalty for their perversion." Once again, the only factor that differentiated the male and female worshipers was castration. The myth regarding Cybele and her young love, Attis, explains the ritual. Apparently, Attis fell in love with a nymph and broke his oath of chastity. Therefore, Cybele killed the nymph which caused Attis to go mad. Attis then mutilated himself and died as a result of the castration. This particular myth was re-enacted every March by the worshipers of Cybele. On the Day of the Blood, a priest of Cybele would be stabbed. After this initial profusion of blood, others would be aroused to give their blood to the goddess. In the midst of loud music, frenzy, dancing, and blood everywhere, younger priests would draw knives and thrust them into their bodies. This hysteria would then spread to the worshipers and many males would join the ranks of the priests by offering their member to the goddess. The ritual was then fully realized when the bloodied priests ran through the streets to throw their cut off member into one of the households. It then became the duty of the household to provide female clothing for these eunuchs who were dedicated to the goddess for the rest of their lives.[206]

A second description that the apostle Paul uses to describe the sexual practices in these cults is through the phrases "exchange of natural relations" or "abandoning natural relations." Paul describes both the male and female sexual practices as such. Many Christians today believe that these references are to homosexuality. In their understanding, both female and male homosexuals are condemned by God because they have abandoned or exchanged heterosexual sex for homosexual sex. It is almost humorous that this scenario is the exact opposite of what the apostle Paul is condemning.

The most common phrase from Romans 1:26 and 27 that is used to condemn homosexuals today is that of going "against nature" which is how the King James Version of the Bible translates verse 26. However, the phrase "against nature" is not used by Paul to refer to homosexuals engaging in sexual lusts, but to worshipers in general, both male and female, engaging in sexual lusts. Also, the word "against" in the Greek is a preposition which does not connote the idea of being in opposition to but rather it means "more than" or "in excess of."[207] And, the word "nature" refers to what is the character of a person or group of persons, what is common—not to a universal law or truth.[208] Paul uses this very phrase in the same epistle in Romans 11:24, describing God's role as acting "against nature" in grafting Christian believers who are wild olive shoots into the Jews who are described as a cultivated olive tree. This helps us to understand that going against nature is not something morally evil, but rather something unusual, uncommon, or an excess.

> I see that all of God's word, from Genesis to Revelation, is consistent in condemning the worship of false gods. The thread throughout Scripture is consistent in God's condemnation of idolatrous practices.

Therefore, what Paul is describing is in fact female worshipers engaging in sexual relations with other women and male worshipers engaging in sexual relations with other males when that is not common for them. In other words, Paul is describing heterosexual persons engaging in same-sex sexual acts. This is an apt description of the practices of the worshipers of Cybele, Aphrodite, Ishtar, or any other deity connected with the fertility cult religions. We have already seen that the cult of Cybele was the first of the eastern religions to arrive in Rome. The Syrian goddess, Cybele, was known as Aphrodite in much of the Greco-Roman world. The main cult of Aphrodite was in Corinth, which is where the apostle wrote Romans. Therefore, it seems that while Paul was in Corinth, viewing the pagan rituals related to Aphrodite, he readily understood what to write in his epistle to the Church in Rome. And, it makes sense that Paul mentions female same-sex acts since this was a common practice among the priestesses of Aphrodite. The rites of the priestesses involved sexual acts among themselves and even a priestess human sacrifice.[209]

It is, therefore, clear that the apostle Paul was not condemning homosexuals or people of same-sex orientation in any of these three New Testament clobber passages. In fact, the apostle Paul condemns idolatrous behavior as it was condemned by God in the Old Testament. The three New Testament clobber passages are understood in the light of cultic worship practices that were prevalent in the New Testament era. I see that all of God's word, from Genesis to Revelation, is consistent in condemning the worship of false gods. The thread throughout Scripture is consistent in God's condemnation of idolatrous practices. Yet, it is a mistake to attempt to apply these condemnations of idolatry to homosexuals or to same-sex sexual relations. It is ludicrous to believe that the apostle Paul would condemn homosexuality in one breath while greeting the household of Narcissus, Nero's famous lover, in the other.[210]

Let us no longer allow the Father of Lies to deceive the Church for another moment about God's love and acceptance for all of God's diverse creation. Make no mistake, there is no place in God's word where homosexuals are condemned. Period. Thankfully, God has been bringing greater revelation of God's word to us through the ages via the work of the Holy Spirit. Every place where God's word has been used as a weapon against people, God seems intent on rectifying the damage with revelation of His heart. This is no less true where God's word has been historically used against homosexual persons. The truth of the matter is God's word affirms God's gay and lesbian children and reveals a special purpose in the heart of God for their lives. Let's allow God's word to not only set people free, but also propel them into fulfilling their destiny.

# 10

# A HIGH CALL

"But God chose the foolish things of the world to shame the wise; God chose the weak things of the world to shame the strong. He chose the lowly things of this world and the despised things—and the things that are not—to nullify the things that are, so that no one may boast before him." ~1 Corinthians 1:27-28

As we untangle the lies that have perverted our understanding of homosexuals, we can only wonder why the enemy would fight so hard to keep a people in bondage. It is because God has a special purpose in mind for His gay and lesbian children. When Jesus went beyond the two known categories of eunuchs in Matthew 19:12 and spoke of a third category, it was divinely inspired. I believe that Jesus, the Son of God, decreed in that moment what God had intended all along for His special gay and lesbian sons and daughters. In fact, Jesus created a third category of eunuchs in order to catapult eunuchs into fulfilling the purpose of God for their lives.

Jesus taught his disciples in Matthew 19:12 that "... there are eunuchs who have made themselves eunuchs for the kingdom of heaven's sake." (NKJV) As mentioned earlier, Jesus here elevated the status of eunuchs in this third category. In the first two categories, Jesus was simply describing to his contemporaries what they would have been familiar with. But,

> In fact, Jesus created a third category of eunuchs in order to catapult eunuchs into fulfilling the purpose of God for their lives.

their eyes must have opened wide when Jesus spoke about those who would make themselves eunuchs for the sake of complete dedication to God's purposes.

The key to this third category of eunuch mentioned by Jesus is in the verb *eunouchizo* which means "to castrate and, metaphorically, to make one's self an eunuch...."[211] This Greek verb is used not just once but twice by Jesus in presenting this third category of eunuch to us. What is strongly suggested here is the making of one's self as a eunuch. In other words, Jesus is highlighting in this third category an act of the will or the aspect of volition.

Jesus created this third category of eunuch as a description of the ideal eunuch. The first two categories were well-known categories of eunuchs. There was common knowledge of the existence of eunuchs who did not choose to be eunuchs but rather were simply born as eunuchs. This type of natural-born eunuch is what we today classify as homosexual or persons of same-sex orientation. There is no choice for the individual in this matter. It is a type of eunuchism that is involuntary, if you will.

Then, the second type of eunuch is one who is made into a eunuch. In this category, we have seen that man-made eunuchs were often involuntarily made into eunuchs. Although, prior to the eighth century BC, there was a long history as well of young men who desired to become castrated due to religious pursuits or in order to obtain a high office. Thus, the man-made eunuch was created by either the individual choosing to become castrated or by someone else imposing castration upon them.

But, this third category of eunuch is something altogether different. After stating what existed in terms of categories of eunuchs, Jesus goes on to present a totally new thing. Jesus here reinstates the original purpose of the eunuch.

In this third category, Jesus states prophetically that there are eunuchs who will make themselves eunuchs for the sake of the kingdom of God. Without a clear understanding of natural-born eunuchs as the Master Designer's creation and man-made eunuchs as an attempt by the master counterfeiter to distort the true meaning and purpose of a eunuch, it would be easy to misunderstand Jesus' comments on this new category of eunuch.

In this third category of eunuch, Jesus certainly was not inviting people to physically castrate themselves, since this would only produce more man-made eunuchs. This notion would have erroneously encouraged individuals to emulate the pagan priests and temple workers who castrated themselves as a way of dedicating themselves to a pagan deity. On the other hand, Jesus' words were also not an invitation for individuals to attempt the impossible task of becoming a natural-born eunuch on their own. We have seen how Jesus and other writers described people of same-sex orientation as born thus from the womb. It is apparent that Jesus was not encouraging heterosexual people to somehow make themselves a different orientation.

> What Jesus offered was an invitation. He made clear that serving God for the kingdom of heaven's sake was of utmost importance and, in fact, spelled out God's agenda for eunuchs.

It is my view that Jesus was making clear here that a eunuch—a true eunuch for that matter—would still have to choose to dedicate themselves to God. In other words, an individual could be a natural-born eunuch, or a person of homosexual orientation through no volition of their own, and still ignore the fact that they are called to be a eunuch for the sake of the kingdom of Heaven. This means that a modern-day eunuch or a person of homosexual orientation might succeed at recognizing their sexuality, but fail at recognizing their Divine purpose. It was revolutionary for Jesus to encourage natural-born eunuchs to "make themselves eunuchs" by going beyond orientation to the fact of their high calling. What Jesus offered was an invitation. He made clear that serving God for the kingdom of heaven's sake was of utmost importance and, in fact, spelled out God's agenda for eunuchs.

Now that we have attempted to search out and understand each of the three categories of eunuchs offered by Jesus, it should be stated that the first category of eunuch is actually the original design of God for eunuchs. In all of humanity, it seems that God has ordained for a small percentage of the human population to be *natural-born eunuchs*. In every society and in every nation, there will always be 3 or 4 percent of the population who are homosexual and this sexuality is not chosen but rather determined in the womb.

> In all of humanity, it seems that God has ordained for a small percentage of the human population to be natural-born eunuchs. In every society and in every nation, there will always be 3 or 4 percent of the population who are homosexual and this sexuality is not chosen but rather determined in the womb.

It is revelational to liken natural-born eunuchs to the first-fruit offering. The first-fruit offering was not the tithe or the 10 percent that was to be given to God. Instead the first-fruit offering was the first and very best of any given harvest. In Israel there are two harvest seasons. The first-fruit offering was a gift given to God of the very best received which would by faith secure a blessing upon the coming harvest. I see that God has given natural-born eunuchs a high calling and a high position. When God looks at His natural-born eunuchs today, I believe He sees a wonderful harvest of all of the nations that are His inheritance. It is beautiful to know that God's modern-day eunuchs are the apple of His eye. Gay and lesbian Christians just need to know this so they can walk in their calling.

The *man-made eunuchs*, on the other hand, are simply a counterfeit or perhaps more aptly put, an artificial attempt at God's original design. Whereas the first category offered by Jesus confirmed God's original design for eunuchs, the third category provides us with the original purpose for eunuchs. It is the calling of God for modern-day eunuchs, who are separated unto God by their sexuality, to dedicate their lives in service to God. We will in this chapter discuss the various ways that modern-day eunuchs are called to dedicate their lives to God.

It is notable that Jesus' remarks about eunuchs are positive considering the current debate about homosexuality in the modern Christian Church. Isn't it interesting that Jesus never spoke about eunuchs in terms of healing, reprogramming, or restoration? In Matthew 19:12 there is no suggestion that a eunuch needs to be fixed, healed, or restored back into society. Remember that Jesus was all too happy to heal the blind, the sick, the oppressed, and to even raise some who were "sleeping" back to the living. But nowhere do we find Jesus healing the eunuch. Rather, to be a eunuch is held up as a model. It is a good thing to be a eunuch. The eunuch, in the context of Jesus' teaching on marriage and divorce, is certainly outside of the heterosexual structure of society. Yet according to Jesus, the eunuch life is a model life and a prestigious calling.

Now let's also take a look at how Jesus' words were misunderstood in the early Church by religious leaders. As the Church was forming, it was influenced on all sides with the reality of castration as a practice of religious devotion. Therefore, it is not surprising that Jesus' words were misunderstood in this context. It is a fact that many of the early Church leaders opted for castration themselves as a way of dealing with their own sexual urges, whether homosexual or heterosexual in nature. Celibacy also has a rich tradition within Christianity. Castration or celibacy was upheld by some as an attempt to dedicate themselves fully to God. One of the most notable Christian leaders who participated in castration was Origen, who later in the third century was labeled heretical. He was a follower of Valentius. This practice of castration amongst Christians became common in Syria and Mesopotamia.[212]

There was widespread teaching during the first few hundred years of Christianity on celibacy, self-castration, and even on sexual abstinence as a requirement of Church membership.[213] Apparently, sexual relations were considered by many as carnal. In some sects of Christianity, sexual relations were not even permitted within the marriage relationship. Instead, there was a high value placed upon spirituality. By the late fourth century and early fifth century, sexual abstinence as a requirement of Church members was rejected by the Church. The Church councils in the fourth century also took a stance against self-castration in order to prevent the loss of Church membership.

Here is how the Council of Nicea handled the issue of self-castration among its clergy in 325 AD:

> If anyone in sickness has undergone surgery at the hands of physicians or has been castrated by barbarians, let him remain among the clergy. But if anyone in good health has castrated himself, if he is enrolled among the clergy he should be suspended, and in future no such man should be promoted. But, as it is evident that this refers to those who are responsible for the condition and presume to castrate themselves, so too if any have been made eunuchs by barbarians or by their masters, but have been found worthy, the canon admits such men to the clergy.[214]

The fact that the 300 bishops at the Council of Nicea had to address the issue of self-castration among the clergy indicates that it was a real problem in the Church at the time. During this time frame, councils in the Church refused celibacy of priests. This didn't last very long, however, because by the late fourth century the Church began to insist on sexual abstinence for priests.[215]

It is clear that some within the Church took Jesus' words literally regarding *eunuchs who make themselves eunuchs for the sake of the kingdom of heaven,* and chose to physically castrate themselves. Others took Jesus' words in a metaphorical sense and opted to refrain from marriage or chose celibacy. "Spiritual eunuchs" desired to remain outside the bonds of marriage so that they could dedicate their lives to the purposes of God. This reasoning is flawed because it perpetuates a negative view of sex and also maintains that celibacy is something chosen rather than a freely given gift of God.

According to the apostle Paul, celibacy is actually a gift of God. In Paul's discussion of appropriate sexual relations, marriage and celibacy in 1 Corinthians 7:1-9, Paul mentions his own gift of celibacy.

> Now concerning the things of which you wrote to me: It is good for a man not to touch a woman. Nevertheless, because of sexual immorality, let each man have his own wife, and let each woman have her own husband. Let the husband render to his wife the affection due her, and likewise also the wife to her husband. The wife does not have authority over her own body, but the husband does. And likewise the husband does not have authority over his own body, but the wife does. Do not deprive one another except with consent for a time that you may give yourselves to fasting and prayer, and come together again so that Satan does not tempt you because of your lack of self-control. But I say this as a concession, not as a commandment. For I wish that all men were even as I myself. But each one has his own gift from God, one in this manner and another in that. But I say to the unmarried and to the widows: It is good for them if they remain even as I am; but if they cannot exercise self-control, let them marry. For it is better to marry than to burn with passion. (NKJV)

Here we see that Paul speaks about the fact that he is unmarried and that it is a gift of God. The word "gift" used by Paul is the Greek word *charisma*[216] which is the same word used to describe the gifts of the Holy Spirit. Charisma connotes spiritual endowment, grace, and miraculous faculty. Needless to say, when celibacy is not a gift of God for someone, there is a lack of miraculous faculty or spiritual endowment connected to the practice.

Interpreting Jesus' words on the third category of eunuch literally (as self-castration) or metaphorically (as reason to remain unmarried or celibate) really misses the point. The early Church bought into these ideas and it only brought confusion. This line of thinking refuses to acknowledge Jesus' comments on natural-born and man-made eunuchs. In offering this third and new category of eunuch, Jesus did not intend to bring bondage for anyone and certainly not for modern-day eunuchs.

When Jesus remarked that there are eunuchs who would make themselves eunuchs for the kingdom of heaven's sake, I don't believe it was in His mind that the Church would begin to enforce celibacy for heterosexuals or for homosexuals. The Christian Church today should learn from its past on enforcing celibacy and sexual abstinence upon its members and reject attempting to justify it now for Christian homosexuals. Also, Jesus' comments about eunuchs should not be a license for the Church to keep homosexuals from covenant relationships nor from appropriate sexual relations within covenant. After all, Jesus came to give life, and abundant life at that. It just does not make sense to continue to promote bondage in sexuality, sexual relations, or in marriage relationships for anyone in the Church. The issue of covenant relationships and marriage equality for everyone in the Church needs to be addressed wisely.

> Needless to say, when celibacy is not a gift of God for someone, there is a lack of miraculous faculty or spiritual endowment connected to the practice.

In conclusion, when Jesus spoke about eunuchs, he redeemed the name and brought clarity regarding God's purpose or agenda for eunuchs. Apparently, Jesus identified natural-born eunuchs and man-made eunuchs in order to make a point beyond their existence at the time. Jesus wanted to reinstate what he knew to be true eunuchs, that is, true eunuchs with a purpose. In Jesus' newly created category of eunuch we see a call to radical devotion for God's gay and lesbian children. Gays and lesbians are a special people with a special calling. They are in fact called to live their lives for the sake or purpose of the kingdom of heaven. This agenda, which comes from heaven, will be accepted by the willing at heart.

Jesus gave the invitation for every gay and lesbian individual to fulfill their destiny in God. There is a Gay Agenda or Divine destiny for those who will hear the high call.

> Gays and lesbians are a special people with a special calling. They are in fact called to live their lives for the sake or purpose of the kingdom of heaven.

# 11

## GOD'S FAVORITE EUNUCHS

"I pray also that the eyes of your heart may be enlightened in
order that you may know the hope to which he has called you...."
~Ephesians 1:18

God is looking for modern-day eunuchs who will fully dedicate
themselves to God. In fact, God has called every believer to
lay down their lives and pick up their cross. All believers are similarly
called to make certain that God is placed first in their lives. We are
all called to love the Lord God with all of our heart, soul, mind, and
strength. Yet some people have a particular calling that leads them to be
more fully set apart than others for the purposes of God.

In the Church, there are many levels of calling, gifting, and
position. For example, in the Church there are leadership roles such
as that of apostle, prophet, teacher, pastor, and evangelist. And, within
the leadership offices there are even combinations of giftings that an

individual can receive from God. Then, God supernaturally endows others within the Church with a variety of different giftings, such as that of helps, administration, mercy, giving, gifts of healing, great faith, and so on. Yet, one type of calling that is often overlooked is that of the modern-day eunuch. Eunuchs are called to a special place in the Church and make up a special rank in the army of God.

Eunuchs are to fulfill their calling both in the Body of Christ and in the world. They make up a special part of the Church. Without modern-day eunuchs, the Church is greatly lacking. Modern-day eunuchs are also called to devote themselves to God's work in the world for the kingdom of heaven's sake. They might have assignments in various spheres in society such as in government, business, education, the media, arts and entertainment, or the family. But, wherever they are directed in their assignment, they are nevertheless called to a certain place of influence, intimacy, commitment, and service to God that is greater than for most. This is the high calling of God that is upon their lives.

> Eunuchs are called to a special place in the Church and make up a special rank in the army of God.

I would like to highlight many of God's servants who were eunuchs. These people were important enough to God that they are included in the Bible and many of them by name. Gay and lesbian Christians can learn from the lives of these eunuchs mentioned in the Bible about how to fully serve God. These ancient eunuchs were set apart for service. Here are examples of some of God's favorite eunuchs.

## Called to influence—*Ebed-Melech*

Eunuchs were employed in royal palaces in a variety of ways. They were set apart in royal palaces in order to serve the royal officials. They would function, depending on their role, at different levels of influence and status. If you served in the presence of a king or queen, it was considered an honor. At the top levels, eunuchs could hold great influence with the royal leader. Sometimes, certain eunuchs would end up being the right-hand person to the royal leader, be it a king or a queen. If the royal leader was to confide in anyone in the palace, often times it was to a eunuch. This afforded some eunuchs great influence as seems to be the case for the eunuch named Ebed-Melech.

In Jeremiah 38:7 we are introduced to Ebed-Melech, the Ethiopian eunuch. He is employed at the royal palace in service to King Zedekiah during the last days before the destruction of Jerusalem. Jeremiah the prophet is prophesying during this time and he is very much disliked by the other prophets and royal advisers. This is because Jeremiah is prophesying that the Babylonians are coming to destroy Jerusalem and God is going to allow this destruction. Certain leaders, including the king's grandson, go to the king and tell him that Jeremiah should be put to death because of his message. They tell the king that Jeremiah is discouraging the soldiers and the people left in the city with his words of doom. In response, King Zedekiah places Jeremiah in the hands of these officials. They take Jeremiah and put him in a cistern in the courtyard of the king's son, Malkihjah. The cistern was filled with mud so when they lowered Jeremiah into it, he sank down into the mud. What a terrible place to be!

This is where Ebed-Melech comes into the picture. His name means "Servant of a King"[217] and we shall see that he served King Zedekiah well, but also more importantly, he was God's faithful servant. Ebed-Melech uses his influence with King Zedekiah and in so doing, becomes an avenue of salvation for the prophet Jeremiah.

Jeremiah 38:7-9 says this of Ebed-Melech:

> Now Ebed-Melech the Ethiopian, one of the eunuchs, who was in the king's house, heard that they had put Jeremiah into the dungeon. When the king was sitting at the Gate of Benjamin, Ebed-Melech went out of the king's house and spoke to the king, saying: 'My lord the king, these men have done evil in all that they have done to Jeremiah the prophet, whom they have cast into the dungeon, and he is likely to die from hunger in the place where he is. For there is no more bread in the city.' (NKJV)

Upon hearing of the prophet Jeremiah's plight, Ebed-Melech sought out the king in order to help Jeremiah. He didn't beg the king in private for the sake of Jeremiah. Instead, he left the royal palace and went right up to the king as he was sitting in his position of authority at the Benjamin Gate. The Benjamin Gate was a very public arena so you can see that this eunuch was confident in approaching the king. It was there that Ebed-Melech entreated the king on Jeremiah's behalf. This fact alone is remarkable considering that it was the king himself who had originally handed Jeremiah over to some wicked officials.

Another important factor in this story is that Jeremiah was literally being held prisoner in the cistern of the king's son. In spite of these facts, Ebed-Melech told the king how these royal leaders had acted wickedly and that Jeremiah would surely die of starvation in the cistern. Ebed-Melech obviously knew that he had great influence with King Zedekiah. If he had not known this he might have opted to use a more subtle approach to the problem at hand. The fact that Ebed-Melech's influence is greater than the other royal officials and even the king's son is seen in the king's positive response to the eunuch in Jeremiah 38:10.

> "Then the king commanded Ebed-Melech the Cushite,
> 'Take thirty men from here with you and lift Jeremiah
> the prophet out of the cistern before he dies.'"

At this point the story gets to be quite humorous. You give a eunuch employed at the royal palace an undercover mission, and it is bound to be a vastly different operation than if a non-eunuch had approached the same task. When Ebed-Melech arrives to rescue Jeremiah from the cistern with thirty men in tow, he also brings with him some old rags and worn-out clothes. Don't ever say that last year's style will not come in handy someday. Ebed-Melech instructs Jeremiah to place the old rags and worn-out clothes under his arms to pad the ropes they use to lift the prophet out of the cistern.

Because of this one eunuch's courage and great influence with the king, Jeremiah the prophet lived and remained in the courtyard of the guard until the day Jerusalem was captured.

It seems that Ebed-Melech's act of delivering the prophet Jeremiah from those wicked men really touched God's heart. So God remembered Ebed-Melech when disaster came to Jerusalem. It tells us in Jeremiah 39, that Jerusalem was destroyed by the Babylonians. Yet at the end of this chapter, God gives Jeremiah a personal word of encouragement to give to Ebed-Melech according to Jeremiah 39:15-18.

> While Jeremiah had been confined in the courtyard of the guard, the word of the Lord came to him: 'Go and tell Ebed-Melech the Cushite, `This is what the Lord Almighty, the God of Israel, says: I am about to fulfill my words against this city through disaster, not prosperity. At that time they will be fulfilled before your eyes. But I will rescue you on that day, declares the Lord; you will not be handed over to those you fear. I will save you; you will not fall by the sword but will escape with your life, because you trust in me,' declares the Lord.

What an awesome act of God to show favor and bring salvation to this one eunuch from the royal palace. Even though the king and most of the other royal officers were destroyed because of their lack of obedience to the word of the Lord, this one eunuch was saved. God made mention of him by name in the Bible because he trusted in the Lord and did what was right. The truth of the matter is that Ebed-Melech had great influence with King Zedekiah. He knew to go to him about the matter with the prophet Jeremiah simply because he understood the king well. Ebed-Melech was not just any servant of the King, but rather, he was a servant held in high esteem. It seems obvious that the king trusted Ebed-Melech implicitly.

Ebed-Melech also had favor and influence with the Living God. What is interesting is that we do not know for certain if Ebed-Melech is a natural-born eunuch or a man-made eunuch. The criteria that we have used to identify natural-born eunuchs in the biblical text is not present in the story of Ebed-Melech. In other words, the Bible does not mention if this particular eunuch is in covenant with God nor does it describe Ebed-Melech as participating in the worship of God.

However, the biblical story does reveal two important factors about Ebed-Melech. First, this eunuch is described as faithful to God's prophet, Jeremiah. He seems to truly care for the prophet of God during the reign of King Zedekiah. And, secondly, when God speaks to Ebed-Melech through the prophet Jeremiah, God specifically says to him, "I will save you… because you trust in me." What a wonderful thing for God to say about anyone! What this indicates is that regardless of whether Ebed-Melech is a natural-born eunuch or a man-made eunuch, he at some point in his life decided to place his faith in God. It is through this wonderful relationship with God that he probably also learned of his true calling as a eunuch.

What we can discover from the life of Ebed-Melech is that some are called to have great influence. The greatest level of influence comes, however, by serving God faithfully. In this story of Ebed-Melech we can see that he was called the *Servant to a King* because he was called to serve King Zedekiah. As it turns out, Ebed-Melech was also privileged to serve God. And, by following this higher calling, Ebed-Melech inherited salvation and received great favor from God.

## Called to intimacy—*Hegai*

Everyone loves the story of Esther. She stood up before the king at a crucial time in the history of the Jews and was God's instrument for their deliverance. The story of Esther would not be complete, however, if not for the whole host of eunuchs that are a part of her life. The role of one eunuch in particular is important for us in understanding intimacy with God.

King Xerxes, the ruler of Persia and Media, was hosting a banquet for all of his officials as well as for all of those in the citadel of Susa. On the seventh day of the banquet, King Xerxes sent seven of his eunuchs to bring to him the Queen so that he might display her beauty to his guests.

> What we can discover from the life of Ebed-Melech is that some are called to have great influence.

148

Unfortunately, Queen Vashti disobeyed the king's request and refused to attend the banquet. As a result, the queen was never again to enter the presence of the king and her royal position was to be given to someone else worthy of the title. This brought about a great search for the right person to be selected as the new queen.

A plan was formulated where beautiful young virgins from every province were sent into the harem at the citadel so that the king could chose for himself the new queen. The eunuch who was in charge of all of the women at the citadel was also given charge of these young virgins. His name was Hegai. Apparently, he was skilled in the care of the women at the palace because he was in charge of them all. This was obviously a position of great honor and of great trust. And now, Hegai was also given charge of the young virgins who would need special care and attention. Hegai knew that one of them would become the new queen. Needless to say, Hegai had a very important job.

It is under Hegai's tutelage that the young virgin, Esther is selected and prepared to become the new queen. Esther 2:8-9 describes the scope of Hegai's care for Esther.

> When the king's order and edict had been proclaimed, many girls were brought to the citadel of Susa and put under the care of Hegai. Esther also was taken to the King's palace and entrusted to Hegai, who had charge of the harem. The girl pleased him and won his favor. Immediately he provided her with her beauty treatments and special food. He assigned to her seven maids selected from the king's palace and moved her and her maids into the best place in the harem.

What is often overlooked in this story is the importance of the eunuchs. This is especially true when it comes to the crucial role that Hegai plays in preparing Esther to become queen. Hegai receives many young virgins under his care, but it is he that selects Esther as the most pleasing. He then spends extra care in preparing her with special food and beauty treatments. This process of selection of Esther by Hegai speaks to more than just Hegai's good job performance as the overseer of the king's harem. It speaks of his intimate knowledge of the king.

Hegai was able to prepare young Esther to be selected as the new queen because he was familiar and intimate with the king. He understood the heart of the king. He also understood the desires of the king. Hegai spent his efforts in preparing Esther to be approved by the king. Even Esther herself appreciated the unique insight and discernment that Hegai alone possessed regarding the king's desires. For she took with her only what Hegai had suggested when she had her meeting with the king as indicated in Esther 2:15-17.

> I see that there are many gay and lesbian Christians who are called by God to prepare the Church to walk in wholeness.

> When the turn came for Esther (the girl Mordecai had adopted, the daughter of his uncle Abihail) to go to the king, she asked for nothing other than what Hegai, the king's eunuch who was in charge of the harem, suggested. And Esther won the favor of everyone who saw her. She was taken to King Xerxes in the royal residence in the tenth month, the month of Tebeth, in the seventh year of his reign. Now the king was attracted to Esther more than to any of the other women, and she won his favor and approval more than any of the other virgins. So he set a royal crown on her head and made her queen instead of Vashti.

This story of Esther is often times likened to the Church and her preparation in becoming the Bride of Christ. For the Church is being prepared as the Bride of Christ to be received one day by Christ Jesus. There is quite a work in progress going on with the Church because God's word has promised that all the spots, wrinkles, and stains will be removed from the Bride. The Church, whatever you might think about her today, is destined to be beautiful, majestic, and glorious.

With this in mind, it is easy to see that the eunuch Hegai is an example of the calling that some modern-day gay and lesbian Christians are to have within the Body of Christ. They are called to be a part of the Church in order to beautify her. Perhaps it is only God's eunuchs who will have the patience and time to deal with all of the spots, wrinkles, and stains. There is no doubt that God's eunuchs will be able to minister healing and restoration to others and especially to those who are in the Church. For who else has received such a grace as modern-day eunuchs? They who once were outcasts have become the people of God. When God's eunuchs are released within the Church there will be great healings and mighty moves of God's Spirit bringing restoration to families, cities, and nations.

In the story of Esther, the king trusted Hegai to care, guard, and protect the women. The biblical story reveals that Hegai was skilled at his work and also highly trusted by the king. As a eunuch, Hegai was not interested in harming or defiling the women he was entrusted to serve. I see that there are many gay and lesbian Christians who are called by God to prepare the Church to walk in wholeness. They are called to train and lead in the Body of Christ and will be entrusted to keep from harm the very people that they serve. In addition, because of the sexual context of the story of Esther in dealing with the preparation of young virgins, I see that it is also the plan of God to release gay and lesbian Christians to promote healthy sexuality and sexual conduct within the Church.

Most importantly, this story of the eunuch Hegai only reinforces the fact that God desires for his modern-day eunuchs to know him intimately. They are called to know the King of Kings by entering into his courts and into his chambers through prayer, praise, and worship. What an opportunity for gay and lesbian Christians to draw near to the Lord and experience his goodness and his glory. God's eunuchs are to be devoted to pleasing the Lord. They are to know the things that are close to the heart of God.

**Called to commitment—two or three eunuchs**

There is a story of a wicked queen named Jezebel in 1 Kings 19 who was thrown from a window by "two or three eunuchs." Jezebel was opposed to God and God's purposes and caused much destruction until her death. Although the eunuchs are nameless, what they accomplished is impressive.

You see, Jezebel was the wife of Ahab, the King of Israel. She influenced the king to turn away from God and to worship false gods. She also killed the prophets of God and set up her own prophets, whom she supported. Ahab, the king, would allow Jezebel to control the kingdom even though he was supposed to be king. When Elijah, the prophet of God confronted the false gods of the land and killed the false prophets, Jezebel vowed to kill him. Elijah ran. This tells you how much influence Jezebel had and the demonic operations that were going on through her life.

Finally, God raised up a young king named Jehu who would go after Jezebel and her household and purge the land of this great sin. In 2 Kings 9, Jehu finally catches up to the woman Jezebel. She attempts to seduce him but fails. This is because Jehu is anointed by God to see Jezebel's rule come to an end. Here is what happened in this spiritual confrontation as described to us in 2 Kings 9:32-33.

> "He [Jehu] looked up at the window and called out, 'Who is on my side? Who?' Two or three eunuchs looked down at him. 'Throw her down!' Jehu said. So they threw her down, and some of her blood spattered the wall and the horses as they trampled her underfoot."

In this story, King Jehu is sent by God on a mission to remove Jezebel from her demonic control over the people. They have a confrontation at Jezreel, where she has planted herself. Jehu looks up at the window and calls out for those who are on his side. Funnily enough, out of all of the people at the palace, only two or three eunuchs peer down. The king then commands these eunuchs to take Jezebel and throw her down to her death. The eunuchs are obedient to King Jehu's command, and she dies a terrible death.

This story of King Jehu in confrontation with the woman, Jezebel, is a picture of spiritual warfare facing the Church today. The name *Jezebel* according to Revelation 2:20, is a description of a demonic principality and not just a name for an individual. The characteristics of this Jezebel demonic spirit are the same characteristics found in the Jezebel mentioned in the Old Testament, but the name no longer just refers to a woman. Rather, the name Jezebel refers to a demonic spirit that likes to operate against the Church. In Revelation 2:20-29, the Church is admonished by Christ Jesus not to tolerate this demonic spirit.

In the Church's spiritual confrontation against this demonic principality, it is important to note that the eunuchs have a role to play. Under the command of the king, or the one in true spiritual authority, the eunuchs can cast down the demonic spirit. This type of spiritual warfare is more and more common in the Church today as the people of God move toward wholeness and begin to fulfill their purpose in the world. Authority to reach the nations will be usurped by this type of demonic presence if it is not dealt with by individuals acting with and under godly authority. It is interesting to see that the eunuchs seem to have a special part in removing this particular demonic principality. I believe it is because the eunuch nation is a nation within every nation. If the reward given by Christ for not allowing this spirit to operate is authority over the nations, then it makes sense that eunuchs are important in this effort. Eunuchs are poised to work within right authority in the Church worldwide to see the kingdom of God spread in every nation.

> Eunuchs are poised to work within right authority in the Church worldwide to see the kingdom of God spread in every nation.

I believe that God is calling godly eunuchs at this time to reach the nations. This type of effort is going to require strict obedience. The "two or three eunuchs" in this incident reveal that it is God's intent to use eunuchs in the Church who will be committed to the Lord. Hopefully, when the King of All asks, "Who is on my side?" there will be a whole nation of eunuch people who will respond with courage and commitment out of their love for God.

Many modern-day eunuchs today ask if their high calling from God is solely a calling for ministry within the Church. They understand that they have been set apart for God's purposes and so they wonder if their gifts are to be used solely within the Church. Let's take a look at the lives of two eunuchs provided for us in the Scriptures who had very different assignments, so we can understand how God may use gay and lesbian Christians in the Church and in the world today.

**Called to the Temple—Nathan Melech**

First of all, we have a description in 2 Kings 23:11 of one eunuch who actually lived at the temple in Jerusalem. His name is Nathan-Melech which means "Given of the King."[218] We do not know from the biblical account exactly what his role was at the temple. I personally believe that Nathan-Melech is a prophetic picture of modern eunuchs who are called to service in the Church. If you are in full-time Church ministry, you probably feel like you live at the Church. To be called by God and assigned to his Church is certainly a high calling. I love what the psalmist wrote about this in Psalm 65:4.

"Blessed are those you choose and bring near to live in your courts. We are filled with the good things of your house, of your holy temple."

When you are a modern-day eunuch called to the house of the Lord, there is nothing else that compares. You love the Church and all that God is doing with his people who are being formed as a dwelling place for God's Spirit.

Again, if we look at the meanings of this eunuch's compound Hebrew name, we find that *Nathan* means "to give, add, supply, appoint, ascribe, and assign"[219] while *Melech* carries the meaning of "a king, and royal."[220] The meaning of *Melech* is better understood when we examine its root word, *Malak,* which means "to reign, to ascend the throne, to induct into royalty, to take counsel, to consult, to be made queen, and to begin to reign or rule."[221]

So, this eunuch was given, added, supplied, appointed, ascribed, or assigned to the temple by the King. It is also apparent from his name that he was also some type of royalty himself. It seems from his name that Nathan-Melech was ruling and reigning under the authority of the king that he served. He ruled and reigned at the temple. It could be that he had oversight of the priests and Levites just as King David had close oversight over the duties and people assigned in the priesthood. King David assigned the Levites to positions of gatekeepers, and singers and musicians at the Tabernacle of David.

Although we might not know his specific duties, what we do know is that Nathan-Melech is an example for modern-day eunuchs who are called to ministry in the Church. Some gay and lesbian Christians too are called by the King of Kings to minister in the Church. They are called to rule and reign in Christ Jesus as they minister first to the Lord and then to others.

## Called to the marketplace—The Ethiopian eunuch

Luke, the writer of the book of Acts, describes the Ethiopian eunuch on his way back home from Jerusalem as "… an important official in charge of all the treasury of Candace, the queen of the Ethiopians."[222] Historically, we know that the queens in Ethiopia were all addressed by the name Candace. This eunuch had a very important position within the royal palace in Ethiopia. He was in charge of the treasury as the finance minister for the government of Ethiopia. And, it seems that he reported to the queen of all of Ethiopia. Now, if the queen was quite wealthy, it could be that this eunuch would have been in charge of overseeing land, vineyards, storehouses, agriculture, the gold and silver, and all of the wealth of the land. There is no doubt that this eunuch had a high position within Candace's palace.

> The Ethiopian eunuch serves as an example to modern-day eunuchs of how God may assign them to the marketplace.

The Ethiopian eunuch serves as an example to modern-day eunuchs of how God may assign them to the marketplace. The royal palace would have been the center of government, business, the judicial system, communications, entertainment, and so forth. Today, we know that God assigns his people to all the spheres of the marketplace. In the past, the royal palace would have been the central place for various spheres to intersect. In ancient times, kings used to sit at the gates of their cities to make proclamations. The gates of cities were also where business transactions took place.

The impact of modern day eunuchs who actually recognize and act upon the call of God upon their lives is yet to be fully seen in the Church and in the world. We are living in an exciting time where God is releasing and raising up his eunuchs for divine purposes. As this occurs, there will be a great move of God's Spirit and a release of the Kingdom of God throughout the nations. Others will find that they have assignments in various spheres throughout the nations. They will be assigned by God to serve in politics, in education, in the media and in other spheres. Most importantly, they will recognize that they are empowered by the Lord as they serve him wherever they are assigned.

However, not every modern-day eunuch will walk in their destiny. It is the call of every eunuch to serve God and please God. Each one has a high calling to fulfill. Yet, not every eunuch will decide to love God and be obedient to him.

A choice must be made to follow after God in the heart of every individual. Likewise, every gay and lesbian person must make a decision to love and serve God. Every modern-day eunuch must make the decision to receive their high calling and walk in it.

In Genesis 40, we see two eunuchs who have very different outcomes in their lives. The chief cupbearer and chief baker were both in jail with Joseph because they had somehow displeased the Pharaoh. Yet, the cupbearer was restored to his position because he had favor with Pharaoh in the end. However, the baker did not fare so well.

In our lives with God, it is always an individual choice to follow him. Eunuchs may have a high call upon their lives but it is nevertheless the choice of every modern-day eunuch to follow that divine destiny or to deny it. The question that must be asked of every gay and lesbian person is this: "Are you ready to be restored into your divine destiny with God or will you reject the God who created you and calls you into His highest?" For every modern-day eunuch, it is my hope that you become one of God's favorite eunuchs.

> Eunuchs may have a high call upon their lives but it is nevertheless the choice of every modern-day eunuch to follow that divine destiny or to deny it.

# 12

## THE PURPOSE OF GOD FOR A EUNUCH NATION

"Arise, shine, for your light has come, and the glory of the Lord rises upon you. See, darkness covers the earth and thick darkness is over the peoples, but the Lord rises upon you and his glory appears over you."
~Isaiah 60:1-2

In my second year of the pastorate, I was invited by my missionary parents to attend an Assembly of God minister's conference at a Church in Brownsville, Florida. The Church was enjoying a tremendous outpouring of the Holy Spirit and I had heard about it. At the time, I was in a place of discouragement as I tried to lead people in my Church into the things of God. Having grown up on the mission-field in Central and South America, I had seen God do extraordinary things all throughout my parent's ministry. I had seen wonderful Spanish speaking people come to a knowledge of God's love and accept Christ in countless numbers. I had also witnessed people in need of physical or emotional healing, deliverance, or the fullness of the Holy Spirit receive what they needed from God over and over again.

Yet, in my own ministry, I felt like I was alone in many ways in an unfamiliar or foreign land. I longed to see God save, heal, deliver, and empower the gay, lesbian, bisexual, and transgender people, along with their families and friends who were in my Church, just as I had witnessed God move in other nations. Yet, it was difficult and spiritually, it was hard ground. I was getting weary and more and more discouraged. Because of this, I agreed to go with my parents to the minister's conference in Florida. I was desperate to know God in a deeper way and to understand God's Spirit and what was lacking in my life and ministry.

While at the minister's conference, I had a powerful encounter with God. Ruth Heflin Ward first ministered in a morning session and the gifts of the Holy Spirit flowed powerfully through her ministry to the people present. Her ministry was always marked by a tremendous move of God's glory. Then, many of us remained for a session on intercessory prayer. It was during this second session that we were all invited to stand and hold hands with those on either side of us as we prayed out loud in unity. It is precious for me to remember how I had my mother's hand on my right and an unknown minister's hand on my left while I cried out with desperation to God. We were all linked together as one and I could hear the sounds of my mother praying next to me. As I prayed in the Spirit it was more sobs and heart cries than prayers that came forth from my lips. During that time, the Holy Spirit showed me in an instant how I was a needed "link" in the Body of Christ and called to be a bridge to others because of my sexuality.

Then, as I prayed in the Spirit, suddenly words started to flow out of my mouth that I understood. I began to weep as I prayed: "Let my people in!" "Let my people in!" I understood in that moment that my cry was similar to the cry of Moses. The intercession the Holy Spirit led me in was for a nation, but it was not necessarily just to bring a nation out of "Egypt" or spiritual oppression. I understood that my calling was also to bring a nation into God's glory. During that conference I was led deeper into the Spirit of God and I experienced God's wonderful glory or presence and power unlike ever before. It left a mark on my life and, of course, it also impacted the Church when I returned. It is one of the reasons why the Church I pastor is called Glory Tabernacle Christian Center. We have encountered God's presence and power and we desire to see God's goodness be known in every life, and in every nation.

> I am convinced that at this time God is not only bringing a eunuch people out of spiritual darkness, but He is also bringing a eunuch people into His glory.

I am convinced that at this time God is not only bringing a eunuch people out of spiritual darkness, but He is also bringing a eunuch people into His glory. There are two things taking place for modern-day eunuchs: God is redeeming them from oppression and then bringing them into His wonderful glory in order to enjoy His presence. From the beginning of time, God set in motion a plan to see all of his creation return to wholeness. It is the heartbeat of God to see every person come into a relationship of intimacy with him. It is my heartbeat to see everyone who has been rejected by people, Churches, or even religion to find their place in Christ.

All throughout the Scriptures we see beautiful pictures of redemption which point to the full redemption that is now available through God's Son, Jesus Christ. Without a Redeemer who can heal the pain, bruises, hurts, weaknesses, and mistakes of the past, we find ourselves stuck in the journey of life. We all need redeeming so that we can move forward in realizing our destiny as individuals and certainly this is true for a eunuch people.

Although we have seen how natural-born eunuchs in Biblical history were involved in covenant relationship and service to God, somewhere along the way this purpose of God for eunuchs was disrupted. Today, if we look back over the current history of gay and lesbian people, we discover that God has been redeeming a people who have been an oppressed people group. You could say that gay and lesbian people have only just recently been established as a people group. A *people group* is a term that simply defines a large sociological grouping of people who perceive themselves to have a common affinity for one another.[223]

Not only can gay and lesbian people be viewed as a people group, they can also be identified as a nation. *Webster's New World Dictionary* defines a nation as "… a stable, historically developed community of people with a territory, economic life, distinctive culture, and language in common; or a people of a territory united under a single government; or a people or tribe."[224] It is clear that gays and lesbians are not a nation defined by a geographical territory, but rather a nation with a distinctive culture.

Gays and lesbians are a tribe, so to speak, uniquely present in every nation. It seems that there are no geographic boundaries for gays and lesbians. I like to explain this phenomenon by saying that gays and lesbians are a nation within every nation. The term *eunuch nation* is also fitting because of the historical aspect of the word *eunuch* which we have seen thus far.

> We all need redeeming so that we can move forward in realizing our destiny as individuals and certainly this is true for a eunuch people.

As we look at this eunuch nation, we need to ask ourselves where and how God has been working in this nation. Relevant questions that need to be asked are: "Is there evidence of God's blessing in this nation's history?" "Is there a pathway of righteousness established?" "Are the gifts of this eunuch nation revealed and flourishing?"

Presently, the eunuch nation is standing at a place of destiny. This nation is discovering how God created gays and lesbians for his glory. It is important for every person to find their purposed destiny and this is no less true for a eunuch nation. So, let's attempt to define the purpose of this nation.

In his book entitled, *Healing America's Wounds*, John Dawson defines the term *Redemptive Purpose* as "The long-term plan of God for any part of creation."[225] The term *Redemptive Purpose* is beneficial because it helps us to see how the original purpose of God for a nation can be altered or tainted somewhere in its history. This is also true for individuals, families, and cities. I believe that this is certainly the case for a eunuch nation. In fact, I see that God is set on bringing a eunuch nation out of oppression, unacceptance, and injustice at this time.

How would we describe the long-term plan of God for this nation? The fact that gays and lesbians are a nation within every nation is a clue to their redemptive

> I like to explain this phenomenon by saying that gays and lesbians are a nation within every nation.

purpose. God saw fit to have a people in every culture and in every nation that are marked by a distinct sexuality. And it is the privilege of these gay and lesbian people to be relieved of many of the responsibilities and obligations that the majority of people possess. Gays and lesbians can be partnered, but in most cases, they will still be free from the responsibilities of raising children. As couples, gays and lesbians remind me of how Jesus sent out His disciples two by two. It is only natural then that gays and lesbians have opportunity to pour their energies more fully into their high calling of serving God and others. They are uniquely able to devote their attention, time, and energy into the pursuit of God and His ways. The assignments of gays and lesbians might lead them to a variety of enterprises. But, the important starting point is to acknowledge that God has placed a high call upon their lives.

Out of every nation or people group, the eunuch nation is exceptionally positioned to devote themselves to God and to impact the world positively.

> Out of every nation or people group, the eunuch nation is exceptionally positioned to devote themselves to God and to impact the world positively.

Also, the fact that the eunuch nation is within every nation provides a remarkable avenue for God to accelerate his purposes in all of the nations. Think about it—if God wanted to bring about a worldwide harvest, he could accomplish it quickly by reaching this one nation that, in turn, could easily reach the geographical nation where they are situated. It is as if God saw a perfect medium for a global harvest when he sprinkled his precious set apart ones across the boundaries of every nation.

Just imagine what it would be like if gays and lesbians in every nation were released into this understanding of their high call. When this begins to be understood, then the gifts that are presently within this nation will be released into the world to be seen by all.

I would like to highlight how John Dawson goes on to further explain God's plan in imparting to each nation its own unique gifts.

> People, cultures, and nations have a redemptive purpose because they bear God-created gifts. They all have a power to bless the world that is an outgrowth of their unique attributes. All that exists is created by God. Satan has never created, and holds no title deed to anything: he is only a creature. God is love, therefore, all that is created serves his ultimate loving purpose: that love be poured out on His creation, and that loving relationship be multiplied throughout time and eternity. Everything created has a purpose, although every purpose is not yet fully understood. Purpose can and will be revealed by our loving Creator; if the knowledge gained will be used lovingly. God's most majestic and important creation is humankind. We are destined for the throne, having the potential of becoming the bride of Christ. We are made in God's own image; therefore, something of God's own nature is revealed through our creation.[226]

If a nation's uniqueness points to its God-given gifts, then certainly it can be said that same-sex orientation is a gift from God. It is beautiful when people see God as the author of the diversity that is present within humanity, which includes sexual diversity. God has purposed that gay and lesbian believers, those who are set apart in their sexual orientation, express their gifts as they fulfill their destiny in God.

Now that we have a clue as to the redemptive purpose of a eunuch nation, let's take a look at how God is moving and revealing His *Gay Agenda* for His eunuch nation.

About forty years ago, there was a major move of God's Spirit when the Rev. Troy Perry was raised up to lead a disenfranchised people into the kingdom of God. Previously a Pentecostal preacher, Troy Perry started the Metropolitan Community Church in Los Angeles, California, as the first Christian Church to welcome and affirm all people regardless of sexuality. The first worship service held in his living room on October 6, 1968, had thirteen people present, of which two were heterosexual.[227] What precipitated the birthing of this Church was God's intervention in Troy's life during a suicide attempt. At the time, the Holy Spirit spoke clearly to Troy affirming that he was loved and fully accepted by God as a gay man. Prior to this landmark occasion, a known homosexual could not worship in any Christian Church or denomination and be fully accepted.

> If a nation's uniqueness points to its God-given gifts, then certainly it can be said that same-sex orientation is a gift from God.

From 1968 to the present, much has happened to reveal God's heart for gays and lesbians. Much scholarship has come forth recently questioning the historical interpretations of biblical texts which have been used to condemn homosexuality. This development of new scholarship in support of homosexuality as a sexuality rather than a sin or a sickness, has caused Churches and denominations to grapple with this issue and enact new policies. An example of an ongoing struggle over homosexuality within a denomination is seen in the schisms that developed within the worldwide Anglican Communion after the Episcopalian Church USA confirmed as bishop the Rev. Gene Robinson, an openly gay man, in 2003.[228]

As far as societal transformation, the Stonewall Riots turned out to be the catalyst that sparked change throughout the United States and globally. This historic event took place in June of 1969, at a gay bar in New York City called The Stonewall Inn. The police and Alcoholic Beverage Control Board agents entered the bar to supposedly look for violations of the alcohol control laws. Apparently, they threw all of the patrons out of the bar one by one after checking identifications and making homophobic remarks. But this time, the gay men, drag queens, students, and other patrons who were there fought back against the harassment. It seems that a parking meter was uprooted, and used to block the door of the bar, trapping the police and agents inside. What ensued was a riot, joining people together for three days as they protested the oppression against homosexuals. The Stonewall Riots mark the beginning of the civil rights movement for gay, lesbian, bisexual, and transgender people in America.[229]

> A eunuch nation is standing at its destiny. It is only now that this mystery of the eunuch calling is being unveiled.

Stonewall was a watershed moment socially for gays and lesbians, just as the birthing of the Metropolitan Community Church nine months earlier had been a spiritual turning point. It is clear that God's grace began to be extended to that particular generation of gay and lesbian people. Also, the establishment of gays and lesbians as a people group or nation took place as a result of these and other events.

God is still working to establish his plan for gays and lesbians. There are blessings being poured out on what is now a second generation movement of gay and lesbian Christians. A eunuch nation is standing at its destiny. It is only now that this mystery of the eunuch calling is being unveiled. It is this calling that is presently being heralded from heaven to bless and empower this new generation of gays and lesbians. The decision to embrace or reject what God is doing will be up to the Church at this time. The Church is at the crossroads. What will it decide?

# 13

## WILL THE REAL CHURCH PLEASE STAND UP?

"On that day I will raise up the tabernacle of David which has fallen down, and repair its damages; I will raise up its ruins, and rebuild it as in the days of old." ~Amos 9:11

This is an exciting time because a new Church is rising up. Heaven has a *Gay Agenda* that is impacting the Church at this time. It will fully be realized in the days to come. A new wineskin is being created as a result of God's handiwork. This new wineskin will contain the new outpouring of God's Spirit for this generation. God is forming the Church into a "House of Prayer" for *all* nations. The one nation that has historically been excluded from God's house is going to be included in this House of Prayer. I believe we are living in a time when the real Church is going to stand up.

It is a defining moment for the Christian Church at this time. I would venture to say that the reputation of the Church is hanging in the balance for this generation of young people. The Barna Group, a research group that studies trends in Christianity, recently discovered that

It is a defining moment for the Christian Church at this time.

non-Christians have an unfavorable view of Christianity. They found this to be especially true with young people today between the ages of sixteen to twenty-nine. Apparently, the vast majority of non-Christians perceive Christianity to be anti-gay, judgmental, and hypocritical.[230] David Kinnaman, the president of the Barna Group, views the Christian Church's reaction to this anti-gay image as the defining response of the Church for this decade.[231]

It is my hope that Christians will take a stand at this time and, hopefully, it will be a stand on the side of love and compassion. I also hope that the Church is courageous enough to take a stand that fully embraces all of God's word rather than religious tradition. Not that the Church should conform to the world but, rather, the Church has to stay flexible enough to hear what the Spirit is saying to the Church. As Jesus spoke about eunuchs in Matthew 19:11 and 12, he said that the message would be accepted by those who can accept it. I believe now is the time for this *Gay Agenda* to be received by the Church. It might seem new to the Church but it doesn't mean it is new to God.

God gives us new things in relationship to His time and when God desires to introduce it back into the Church. Right now, God is giving the Church back something that it has lost. Natural-born eunuchs were a part of the people of God historically. This means that gays and lesbians historically had the favor of God upon them and lived lives in covenant with God. When we see something in the Scriptures that we perhaps never saw before, it might be new to us. Yet, it is not new to God. The Church's defining moment is taking place and so now more than ever, it is time for Christians to embrace what God is reinstating in the earth.

The Church will win out in the end. There is no doubt about that. Christ is building His Church and so we will become a Church without spot or wrinkle. This is Christ's Plan A. There is no Plan B or Plan C with God regarding His Church. All of God's eggs are in this basket, so to speak, and so we have a responsibility to this generation and to future generations. We can't live in fear, ignorance, or with cultural blinders. The real question is, "How long will it take for the Church to line up with God's heart and God's word on the issue of homosexuality?"

Historically, the Church lost out on a great opportunity when in 1271, Nicolo and Matteo Polo arrived in the East. The father and uncle of Marco Polo met with the Kublai Khan who was the world ruler over China, India, and all of the East. The Kublai Khan was interested in the story of Christianity and so he sent them back to their home country with a letter inviting one hundred educated men to come and

> Right now, God is giving the Church back something that it has lost. Natural-born eunuchs were a part of the people of God historically.

teach on Christianity. Unfortunately, it took many years for this to take place and only a few missionaries were ever sent.[232] I believe that God's purpose for the East was frustrated at that time and a harvest of souls for the kingdom of God was lost. It is possible for this failure of the Church to be repeated at this time. However, I trust that the real Church is standing up and it is this Church who will capture the hearts of this generation with God's message of love and truth.

The good news is that Jesus Christ is in charge of building His Church. It is a good thing that He is, because if someone else were in charge, we might see a very different outcome. Jesus made a promise regarding the Church that He is building. He said that even the highest councils of hell would not win against it.[233] Let's face it, the forces of hell have tried to keep the doors of the Church shut to sexual minorities. This is why God is doing some shaking up within the Church today.

All throughout this great building project called the Church, Christ has taken the opportunity to remove things that some people have tried to attach illegitimately to it. We can certainly learn some vital lessons for today from the two examples we have in the Scriptures of Jesus cleansing the temple.

At the beginning of his ministry, Jesus went to Jerusalem for the Jewish Passover. When he saw the temple court area turned into a market place for buying and selling, Jesus' ministry turned into a demolition ministry. It tells us in John 2:13-17, that Jesus made a whip out of cords and with it he drove out all of the cattle, sheep, doves, money changers, and those selling doves. He became a Harrison Ford-type character in order to remove the "raiders" of the ark, if you will. He told the people, "How dare you turn My Father's house into a market!"[234] Righteous zeal consumed Jesus for the house of his Father.

Many today in the Church have zeal but it is mistaken zeal. They are cleansing the Church of people that they do not consider acceptable, thinking that they are in step with Jesus. Yet, I believe that if we want to be in step with what God is doing, we need to open our hearts to those who have historically been considered "unacceptable." Jesus always was drawn to the marginalized, while at the same time opposing the religious.

> Let's face it, the forces of hell have tried to keep the doors of the Church shut to sexual minorities.

Let me draw your attention to the incident where Jesus cleansed the temple at the end of His ministry because it speaks volumes concerning God's heart for his gay and lesbian children. In Mark 11:15-17, it says that Jesus entered the temple and once again drove out those who were buying and selling there. We are told that Jesus ruined the businesses of the money changers and those selling doves.

It seems that both the money changers and the dove vendors were hindering the work of God at that time. They were masters at oppressing the people who came to the temple in order to worship God. The money changers had a business because the priests would not accept offerings from the people unless it was in shekels. Most people came with Roman coinage which was deemed unclean by the priests. The people who came to worship God and give their offerings were forced to have their coins changed into acceptable coinage. The money changers only too gladly assisted in this matter because they charged exorbitant rates.

The dove vendors, however, were even more heartless than the money changers. The reason for this is that the people who came to the temple to offer a dove as an offering to the Lord were poor. At the expense of the poor, the priests and the dove vendors worked together to take advantage of them. First, the priests would find the dove presented to them as unacceptable for one reason or another. Then the priests would direct the individual to the dove vendors. These dove venders would then turn around and sell a "kosher" dove for a lot more money to the poor and split the profits with the priests. So, Jesus removed these people and activities from his Father's house.

Just as Jesus cleansed the temple during his earthly ministry, be assured that today this same demolition activity is taking place. Christ is removing ungodly things and people from the Church today so that the Church can be built up, made strong and beautified. The "money changers" and "dove venders" reveal to us those that Christ is vehemently against. They represent those who take advantage of people who come to Church with the intent of worshiping God. Also, it is the "money changers" and "dove venders" of today who are in the business of illegitimately misusing the financial gifts of God's people for their own personal gain. What is more, they hinder and deny access to certain people who are crying out to God. The bottom line is they represent religious people who judge the worship and sacrifices of others as unacceptable.

What is remarkable is that when Jesus cleansed the temple of all those who were hindering and blocking the true work of God, he was envisioning the Church of today. You see, Jesus made a very prophetic statement as he cleansed the temple. Jesus said: "Is it not written: 'My house will be called a house of prayer for all nations? But you have made it a den of robbers.'"[235]

It is no mistake that when Jesus cleansed the temple He quoted the very words of Isaiah the prophet found in Isaiah 56:7. Yes, Jesus echoed the very words of Isaiah when he decreed that one day eunuchs and foreigners would be gathered together in God's house. Jesus spoke this prophetic declaration as he cleansed the temple in order to confirm that the day had come for God's eunuchs to find their place in God. In the same way, it is time for the Church to welcome and help God's eunuchs discover the "X" or the place that has been reserved for them.

What is the nation that God has his eye on right now? It is the gay and lesbian nation that is spread out in every nation. God is reaching out to this nation and welcoming them and bringing life to them. The gay and lesbian nation is finding its place in the Church as people experience the love of God. In many ways you could say that Christ has a whip and is removing that which hinders, judges, and hurts God's people. Today, Jesus Christ is making a way for leaders of the Church to understand that His gay and lesbian children are included in this house of prayer for all nations.

> Today, Jesus Christ is making a way for leaders of the Church to understand that His gay and lesbian children are included in this house of prayer for all nations.

A crisis can be seen as a problem or as an opportunity. Is the Church in crisis? I believe that the Church is facing a great opportunity whereby many lives can be touched by the love of God. Internal crisis and evaluation is always good in the Church because it keeps the Church in step with new revelation and also relevant to what God is doing in the earth.

One way of looking at this defining moment in history is to see how the first Church dealt with its crisis. In Acts 15 we have the "minutes" if you will, of the first council meeting of the Church. A heated debate took place concerning the Church's stance on Gentile Christians. They struggled, to be honest, with inclusiveness.

The mostly Hebrew Christians had a difficult time accepting the Gentile Christians who were coming to know Christ Jesus through the ministry of Paul and Barnabas. The Hebrew Christians had been brought up in Judaism to believe that Gentiles were unclean. They also didn't like the fact that many of the religious traditions they grew up with under the Law of Moses (such as circumcision) were not being upheld by these Gentile believers. Paul and Barnabas were planting Churches and telling the believers not to worry about being circumcised. Other Hebrew Christians were traveling around to these new converts and bringing confusion to them by telling them they were not saved unless they were circumcised. The situation then in the early Church is very reminiscent of how some Churches today accept gay and lesbian Christians while others are preaching an anti-gay message. A council was held in Jerusalem among the elders and apostles to resolve the issue.

What I find remarkable about this first council meeting of the early Church is that the issues discussed back then still apply to the Church today. First, Peter stood up and told the elders that God accepted the Gentiles because God gave them the Holy Spirit. This very truth is the same today. God is pouring out God's Spirit upon gays and lesbians too. When Peter saw the Spirit of God being poured out upon the house of Cornelius in Acts 10 as the people spoke in tongues and praised God, he could no longer hold onto his religious traditions. Instead, Peter welcomed the Gentile believers into the Church through water baptism. The Church today needs to follow Peter's lead and acknowledge that when the Holy Spirit fills gay and lesbian Christians, it is irrefutable evidence of God's grace and favor.

In fact, Peter stated some pretty remarkable things. Let's take a look at what he said at this council in Jerusalem as recorded in Acts 15:7-11.

> After much discussion, Peter got up and addressed them: Brothers, you know that some time ago God made a choice among you that the Gentiles might hear from my lips the message of the gospel and believe. God, who knows the heart, showed that he accepted them by giving the Holy Spirit to them, just as he did to us. He made no distinction between us and them, for he purified their hearts by faith. Now then, why do you try to test God by putting on the necks of the disciples a yoke that neither we nor our fathers have been able to bear? No! We believe it is through the grace of our Lord Jesus that we are saved, just as they are.

Peter understood that the Gentile Christians were saved by grace just as the Hebrew Christians were saved by grace. The religious traditions, such as following the Law of Moses, had nothing to do with salvation. And more importantly, Peter saw that asking the Gentile Christians to follow the Law of Moses and specifically, circumcision, was actually a yoke to them. Peter stated that even they themselves, the Hebrew Christians, could not keep the Law, so why would they ask a Gentile to try?

This early Church conflict reminds me so much of the way the Church today has treated gay and lesbian Christians. Historically, the modern Church has denied gay and lesbian people inclusion. This is what the Hebrew believers did to the Gentile Christians until finally God released apostles like Peter, Paul, and Barnabas to open up the door of the Church. Think for a moment about how amazing it was for an evangelist like Philip to be led by the Holy Spirit in order to minister to a eunuch. Philip probably didn't understand at the time that God was doing a great work for a eunuch nation in that moment.

Today, it is often times a different story for gays and lesbians in the Church. If gays and lesbians are accepted in many Churches today, it is because they agree to take on a "yoke." Many gay and lesbian Christians have agreed to live celibate lives in order to be included within the Church. Some have sadly left partners which they were in covenant with. Others have avoided relationships all together because they have been influenced to choose celibacy by well-meaning Christians. The problem here is that most heterosexual Christians would not be able to live a life of celibacy either if they were asked to do so as a requirement of Church membership. Celibacy is a yoke upon anyone except those who have been given the gift of celibacy by the Holy Spirit.

> It is sad to see the types of "yokes" that have been placed upon gay and lesbian Christians.

It is sad to see the types of "yokes" that have been placed upon gay and lesbian Christians. Some have agreed to go through ex-gay counseling whereby the yoke of behavior modification is placed upon their necks even though they know deep-down inside that their sexuality is still homosexual. Almost worse, some gays and lesbians have agreed to take on the yoke of hiding their sexuality because they have been asked by their pastors to do so. Usually this duplicity is promoted by the pastor so that the pastor can still use the gifts of the homosexual person without having to deal with the issue of homosexuality with the whole congregation. Perhaps, these Churches and pastors need to examine how the early Church dealt with inclusion. Don't we all believe that salvation by faith is a gift of God? Shouldn't we throw out the religious yokes that keep people in bondage and start promoting freedom in Christ Jesus instead?

This early Church council on inclusion ends in a fabulous way. At the end of all of the discussion, the apostle James seals the deal by quoting from the prophet Amos. In the midst of the Church's first crisis, James quotes Amos' words about God rebuilding the Tabernacle of David.

> "The words of the prophets are in agreement with this, as it is written: 'After this I will return and rebuild David's fallen tent. Its ruins I will rebuild, and I will restore it, that the remnant of people may seek the Lord, and all the Gentiles who bear my name, says the Lord, who does these things that have been known for ages.'" ~Acts 15:15-18

There is a reason why the Holy Spirit led the apostle James to this prophetic word in the midst of such a heated debate. We can learn much today about what God is doing in the Church and the agenda that is on His heart by looking at the promise of God through the prophet Amos. It seems that the Church that Christ is committed to building is patterned after the Tabernacle of David. The Tabernacle of David existed for thirty-three years in Mount Zion. It was amazing because it was ahead of its time. It is a picture of New Testament worship taking place under the Old Testament covenant. David saw ahead of his time to the blood of the Lamb that was shed from the foundations of the earth. Because of this prophetic understanding, David entered the holy of holies through the sacrifice of praise instead of the usual blood sacrifice. The Tabernacle of David is also a model for the Church today in that it was a place of inclusiveness.

One of the main characteristics of the Tabernacle of David was that everyone was welcome to worship God there. Whether Jew or Gentile, rich or poor, young or old, all were welcome at the Tabernacle of David. This is because David set up a tent where the ark of the covenant was seen by everyone who was willing. The Tabernacle's thirty-three years of existence on Mount Zion correlates exactly with Jesus' lifespan, when the glory of God dwelt or tabernacled in his son. John 1:14 states: "The Word became flesh and made his dwelling among us. We have seen his glory, the glory of the One and Only, who came from the Father, full of grace and truth."[236] When you approached the Tabernacle of David to worship, the presence and power of God was available to you.

The Tabernacle of David featured a tent where there was no veil hiding the ark from the people. This type of worship was ahead of its time because the veil was torn away from the Holy of Holies for good later at the death of Christ Jesus on the cross. The glory of God was available for thirty-three years for the all people to see, experience and enjoy at the Tabernacle of David and during the lifetime of Jesus of Nazareth. This is the kind of freedom and inclusivity that God is calling His Church to live out.

The first Church council meeting ended up being a success because the early Church took the opportunity to embrace the Gentile Christians without placing any hindrances upon them. Through inspiration of the Holy Spirit the apostle James was given wisdom from God on how to handle this first Church crisis. James was directed by the Holy Spirit to the prophecy of Amos about what God is building. The Tabernacle of David that is being rebuilt is the same Church that Christ is building today. Christ is committed to building His Church and it is modeled after David's tent. The important characteristic of David's tent that the Church needs to embrace today is the aspect of inclusiveness.

The real Church that Christ is building is where the "whosoever" can come and belong. God longs for people to experience His wonderful love through His Church. Anything that is religious or judgmental or that produces bondage is in opposition to this. As this real Church stands up today by ministering and welcoming all people, then a great acceleration of kingdom harvest will take place.

The challenge of the Church today is to bear the mark of the Savior, Jesus. It is time for the Church to open up its hands wide, as Jesus did on the cross, and welcome all those who will come. The mark of a true Tabernacle of David Church is its inclusiveness which brings down the blessings of God. God is looking for a people who will hunger after God in worship and then hunger to share this love with others. No judgment. No bondage. No restrictions. Just love.

> What kind of Church do you envision? Is it the same kind of Church that Christ envisions?

What kind of Church do you envision? Is it the same kind of Church that Christ envisions? Is it a Church where modern-day eunuchs are fully integrated and using their gifts along with their families and friends? Is it a Church where the walls of division and ignorance are removed and God's *Gay Agenda* is embraced? Is it a Church that actively seeks out the oppressed so that others will see this wonderful attribute of God and fall in love with the Church? I believe that as the Church embraces God's *Gay Agenda*, then it will be catapulted into God's greater agenda. That is, the glory of the Lord revealed in all peoples, tribes and tongues. Now, that is God's ultimate agenda.

# Epilogue

## Let The Wedding Bells Ring!

"…For He has clothed me with garments of salvation and arrayed me in a robe of righteousness, as a bridegroom adorns his head like a priest, and as a bride adorns herself with her jewels." ~Isaiah 61:16b

As a pastor, I know that some of the most precious times in the life of a Church family are when the family comes together to celebrate life through weddings, baby dedications, water baptisms, or the passing of a loved one. These events are special because they bring individuals, couples, and families together in the context of the larger Church family. These significant transitional times in life afford the Church family an opportunity to honor, respect, celebrate, and acknowledge the transitions, as well as participate in them. Of all of these, I do not know which one I would consider a favorite, but certainly weddings are a time of great joy. After all, wasn't it at the marriage of Cana that Jesus performed his first miracle? And, wasn't this first miracle the turning of water into wine?

This tells me that God is concerned about our celebrations and wants to make sure that we enjoy them to the fullest.

This brings us to the question of what Jesus would do today at a same-sex wedding. Would he turn the water into wine and bless the occasion or would he send his regrets and not attend? What is Christ's vision for His Church when it comes to marriage for all those that love one another? If the Church is called to embrace all people including gays and lesbians, then can the love of same-sex couples be celebrated? I wonder if there is celebration in heaven whenever a same-sex couple comes before God in marriage and declares, "I do." In fact, God is pleased when same-sex couples gather in a Church in order to have their pastor, families, friends, and Church family validate and celebrate their love.

On May 9, 2012, the President of the United States affirmed same-sex marriages in a televised interview.[237] President Barak Obama is the first President of the United States to do so. Although no laws were changed because of the President's personal stand in affirming marriage equality, it certainly opened up the door for much discourse on the issue.

One of the traditional views against marriage equality is based in the understanding that allowing gays and lesbians to marry would change the definition of "marriage." After all, marriage historically has always been understood as a transaction between one man and one woman. It is also thought that marriage is only ordained by God for one man and one woman. So, one must ask, what is the definition of marriage?

Interestingly enough, *Unger's Bible Dictionary* relates that the word *marriage* is not found in the Scriptures.[238] Unger indicates that there is no single word in the Bible which refers to marriage or the abstract idea of wedlock. Instead, it seems that words and phrases such as "master," "to take a wife," "to dwell together," "to contract," "to perform the duty of a brother" and the like make reference to what we call marriage today. It is especially difficult for Christians to understand that in reality much of what we have been taught in regards to traditional marriage is in fact rooted in culture. It is necessary for us to dig deeper if we want to embrace God's heart on the issue of intimate relationships.

You can be certain that people today would reject much of the "traditional" marriages that are provided for us in the Bible. Within the first few verses of Scripture we find one traditional marriage model provided for us but it is a polygamous model. In Genesis 4:19, we see that Lamech had two wives. What is even more confusing for many people to acknowledge is that God seemingly approved of polygamous relationships under the Law of Moses.[239] Abraham, the father of our faith, had a wife in Sarah and then, later, a second wife in Hagar. This pattern of polygamy is found in many of the ancient relationships such as with Esau, Jacob, Gideon, Solomon, and others. In fact, Solomon had 700 wives and 300 concubines.

It is apparent from the Scriptures that God seems to have stamped His approval upon a variety of types of marriages which were considered "traditional" in biblical history. A wonderful study on "traditional" marriages provided by Richard Brentlinger in *Gay Christian 101* presents that besides the polygamous marriages, there existed under God's blessing the levirate marriages, mixed marriages, slave marriages, and prisoner-of-war marriages.[240] All of these "traditional" marriages would be shunned today in the Church and in most Western societies. The levirate marriage meant that a brother-in-law was expected to marry a widowed sister-in-law if there was no child from the deceased husband. This was adopted in order to continue the lineage of the deceased brother. It was this type of levirate marriage that Jesus was questioned about by the Sadducees according to Mark 12:18-25. The Sadducees, who did not believe in the resurrection, asked Jesus how many husbands a woman would have in heaven if she had been married by seven brothers in the custom of the levirate marriage. Jesus replied to them as follows in verse 25: "When the dead rise, they will neither marry nor be given in marriage; they will be like the angels in heaven."

As far as slave marriages, we have the example of Abraham and Sarah's slave Hagar as one model. It says in Genesis 16:3:

"So after Abram had been living in Canaan ten years, Sarai his wife took her Egyptian maidservant Hagar and gave her to her husband to be his wife."

In this marriage, Hagar did not have any rights as she was a slave. This verse states that Sarah, who owned the slave girl, gave the woman to her husband in order to be his wife. Another example of slave marriages is described in Exodus 21:1-6. Here it states that under the Law of Moses if a male slave comes to his master with a wife, after the seven years of work he can be released with his wife. However, if the male slave is given a wife by the master, then when the seven years are over, the wife and any children remain the possession of the master. For Christians today, these laws seem cruel yet they were laws that were given by God to the people in that ancient culture.

To me, the most unusual mandate for marriage in the Scriptures is found in the prisoner-of-war marriage that is described in Numbers 31:1-18. Here, God instructs the Hebrew nation to go to war with the Midianite nation. God also instructs the Hebrew men to destroy all of the people with the exception of the Midianite virgin women. The virgins are to be taken by the men for themselves. Yes, this type of marriage seems barbaric for us to today, but it was nevertheless something that God ordained in that ancient culture.

Perhaps this is why when Jesus was questioned about divorce by the religious leaders of his day in Matthew 19, he spoke of God's original intent for marriage as described in Genesis 2:24. Jesus went back to the "beginning" and described God's original purpose in bringing two people together to become one. Although the word "marriage" is not used, this is our model for marriage. It is the ideal marriage, I believe, from God's perspective. We can also learn from Jesus' teaching in Matthew 19 on divorce that God allowed certain procedures under the Law of Moses for divorce because the people's hearts were hard. It seems that all throughout human history, God has attempted to work within culture to bring about the best for people and ultimately, His ideal for intimate relationships. There is certainly a distinction between this ideal of God for intimate relationships and what we know to have been the law or even marriage models as detailed in the Bible.

What is helpful for us today is to understand that according to Jesus, the "becoming of one flesh" referring to the Genesis account, is God's ideal. I think we can all agree on this point. This then allows us to question who is able to participate in God's ideal of intimate relationships. Is the Genesis account of a man and a woman becoming one flesh what God had in mind for all time?

I see the Genesis account of God's ideal of intimate relationships simply set within the context of an explanation of the origins of humankind. The Genesis account describes how God created the earth and humanity and then how humanity populated the earth. Within this context, it would be absurd to expect to see a same-sex relationship described. This Genesis account also does not describe the levirate marriage either or it would have had to state something to the effect of: "For this reason a man will leave his father and mother and be united to his wife and the two will become one flesh until his brother dies leaving no child and he is also united to his sister-in-law."

So, let's get down to the basics and see what actually constitutes God's ideal of intimate relationships. God's ideal for intimate relationships can be described in the word "covenant." God is a covenant God and, therefore, He has established covenant relationships for human beings as well. When two people are in love and called to live life together, they can enter into a covenant of love together. This is the kind of relationship that God participates in and blesses. This is the kind of relationship that Naomi and Ruth enjoyed. Their intimate relationship of love was outside the bounds of a culturally based "marriage" of property and spousal rights, but it was nevertheless an intimate relationship which God honored. In the same way, David and Jonathan enjoyed a covenant relationship of love. Both men were engaged in marriages as prescribed by their ancient culture. Yet, the one love that David valued the most was Jonathan's love. David said of Jonathan in 2 Samuel 26b: "Your love for me was wonderful, more wonderful than that of women."

The proper perspective on intimate relationships is this: they are ordained by God when two people come together in selfless love and dedicate themselves to one another. This is the ideal for intimate relationships which is in accordance with the Genesis account and the New Testament Scriptures. The term *marriage* must be viewed as a term that is engrained in culture and, therefore, not always indicative of God's ideal for intimate relationships. This is why marriages throughout the years have had many different types of configurations. On the other hand, it seems that in the heart of God, there is a covenant relationship of intimacy that is possible for two people who are called to live life together as a couple. I believe this very intent for the union of two persons is possible with two persons of the same-sex.

According to Jesus, there will not be marriage in heaven among the human race. In fact, marriage is something that is temporal or earthly and not eternal. It is something that God has intended for the human race to enjoy, because God has created individuals, for the most part, to be in intimate relationships. It is how humans are wired. Doesn't God start out by saying in Genesis 2:18, "It is not good for the Adam to be alone?" We know that God created the "Adam" as male and female. This means that it is not good for any person to be alone. The majority of humanity will be called by God to enjoy an intimate relationship of love. It is time that we embrace what God intended for all people. It is time for the Church to take a stand for love and covenant. I, for one, believe it is time to let the wedding bells ring for everyone—including for same-sex couples.

# STUDY & DISCUSSION QUESTIONS

You are invited to make the most of the *God's Gay Agenda* Study & Discussion Questions which are available for individuals, friends, and small groups. Please see the website for more information at www.godsgayagenda.com. The Study & Discussion Questions available online are designed to complement the book. To maximize the impact of the study, each participant should have a copy of the book. The Study & Discussion Questions designed for each chapter of the book are a vital part of the learning experience. The questions will help individuals or small groups to more fully absorb the subject matter. They will also promote thoughtful and lively interaction for small groups.

# BIBLIOGRAPHY

Arthur, L. Robert. *The Sex Texts: Sexuality, Gender and Relationships in the Bible.* Omaha, NE: Arthur, 1994.

*Babylonian Talmud.*

Besen, Wayne. *Anything But Straight: Unmasking the Scandals and Lies Behind The Ex-Gay Myth.* New York and London: Harrington Park Press, 2003.

Blair, Ralph. *Homosexualities, Faith, Facts and Fairy Tales.* New York: Blair, 1991.

Blanchard, R., and A. F. Bogaert. "Homosexuality in men and the number of older brothers." *American Journal of Psychiatry* 153 (1996): 27-31.

Blanchard, R., and Lee Ellis. "Birth weight, sexual orientation and the sex of preceding siblings." *Journal of Biosocial Science* 33 (2001): 451-467.

Blanchard, R., J. M. Cantor, A. F. Bogaert, S. M. Breedlove and L. Ellis. "Interaction of fraternal birth order and handedness in the development of male homosexuality." *Hormones and Behavior* 49 (2006): 405-414.

Boswell, John. *Christianity, Social Tolerance, and Homosexuality: Gay People In Western Europe from the Beginning of the Christian Era to the Fourteenth Century.* Chicago and London: University of Chicago Press, 1980.

*Same-Sex Unions In Premodern Europe.* New York: Villard Books, 1994.

Brentlinger, Richard. *Gay Christian 101: Spiritual Self-Defense For Gay Christians.* Pace, FL: Salient Press, 2007.

Bromiley, Geoffrey W. *Theological Dictionary of the New Testament: Abridged In One Volume.* Edited by Gerhard Kittel and Gerhard Friedrich. Grand Rapids: William B. Eerdmans, 1985.

Brooten, Bernadette. *Love Between Women: Early Christian Responses to Female Homoeroticism*. Chicago and London: University of Chicago, 1996.

Bullough, Vern. "Eunuchs In History And Society." Chap. 1 in *Eunuchs In Antiquity And Beyond*, edited by Shaun Tougher, 1-18, London: Classical Press of Wales and Duckworth, 2002.

*Sexual Variance in Society and History*. Chicago and London: University of Chicago Press, 1976.

Clement of Alexandria. *Paedagogus*.

Clement of Alexandria. *The Stromata*.

Dawson, John. *Healing America's Wounds*. Ventura, CA: Regal Books, 1994.

De Cecco, John P. and David Allen Parker. "The Biology of Homosexuality: Sexual Orientation or Sexual Preference?" Chap. 1 in *Sex, Cells and Same-Sex Desire: The Biology of Sexual Preference*, edited by John P. De Cecco and David Allen Parker. New York: Harrington Park Press, 1995. 1-28.

Edwardes, Allen. *Erotica Judaica: A Sexual History of the Jews*. New York: Julian Press, 1967.

Ellis, Lee and M. Ashley Ames. "Neurohormonal functioning and sexual orientation: A theory of homosexuality- heterosexuality." *Psychological Bulletin* 101, no. 2 (1987): 233- 258.

Ferguson, Everett. *Backgrounds of Early Christianity,* 2nd ed. Grand Rapids: WM. B. Eerdmans, 1993.

Fletcher, Lynne Yamaguchi. *The First Gay Pope and other records*. Boston: Alyson Publications, 1992.

Frangipane, Francis. *This Day We Fight!: Breaking The Bondage of A Passive Spirit*. Grand Rapids: Chosen Books, 2005.

Goldberg, B. Z. *The Sacred fire: The Story of Sex In Religion*. New York: Garden City, 1930.

Greenberg, David. *The Construction of Homosexuality*. Chicago and London: University of Chicago, 1988.

Gregory of Nazianzus. *Oration*.

Guthrie, D., J. A. Motyer, A. M. Stibbs, and D. J. Wiseman, eds., *The New Bible Commentary Revised.* Grand Rapids: WM. B. Eerdsmans, 1970.

Helminiak, Daniel A. *What the Bible Really Says About Homosexuality.* New Mexico: Alamo Square Press, 2000.

Horner, Tom. *Jonathan Loved David.* Philadelphia: Westminster Press, 1978.

Humana, Charles. *The Keeper of the Bed: The Story of the Eunuch.* London: Arlington Books, 1973.

Josephus. *Antiquities of the Jews.*

Kepner, Jim. *Becoming A People... a 4,000 year gay and lesbian chronology.* Hollywood, CA: The National Gay Archives, 1983.

Kinnaman, David and Lyons, Gabe. *UnChristian, What A New Generation Really Thinks About Christianity... And Why It Matters.* Grand Rapids: Baker Books, 2007.

Kroeger, Catherine. "The Apostle Paul and the Greco-Roman cults of Women." *Journal of the Evangelical Society* 30 (March 1987): 25-38.

Leupold, Herbert C. *Exposition of Genesis,* Vol. 1 of *Leupold on the Old Testament.* Grand Rapids: Baker Book House, 1953.

Mader, Donald. "The Entimos Pais of Matthew 8:5-13 and Luke 7:1-10." In *Homosexuality and Religion and Philosophy*, edited by Wayne R. Dynes, 223-235, New York: Garland, 1992.

Malik, Faris. "Born Eunuchs: Homosexual Identity in the Ancient World." Unpublished Manuscript, last modified March 1, 1999. Microsoft Word file.

Martin, Dale, B. "Arsenokoites and Malakos: Meanings and Consequences." Chap. 8 in *Biblical Ethics & Homosexuality: Listening to Scripture*, edited by Robert L. Brawley, 117-136, Kentucky: Westminster John Knox Press, 1996.

McNeill, John J . *The Church and the Homosexual.* Kansas City: Sheed, Andrews, and McMeel, 1976.

Miner, Jeff and John Tyler Connoley. *The Children Are Free: Reexamining the Biblical Evidence on Same-sex Relationships*. Indianapolis: Jesus Metropolitan Community Church, 2002.

Mitamura, Taisuke. *Chinese Eunuchs: The Structure Of Intimate Politics.* Translated by Charles A. Pomeroy. Rutland, VT and Tokyo: Charles E. Tuttle, 1963.

Morris, Leon. *Luke: An Introduction And Commentary.* The Tyndale New Testament Commentary. Illinois and England: Intervarsity Press, 1974.

Mustanski, Brian S., Michael G. DuPree, Caroline M. Nievergelt, Sven Bocklandt, Nicholas Schork, and Dean Hamer. "A genomewide scan of male sexual orientation." *Human Genetics* 116, no. 4 (2005): 272-278.

Myers, David G. *Exploring Psychology.* 6th ed. New York: Worth, 2005

Nanda, Serena. *Neither Man nor Woman: The Hijras of India.* Belmont, CA: Wadsworth, 1990.

Nissinen, Martti. *Homoeroticism in the Biblical World.* Translated by Kirsi Stjerna. Minneapolis: Fortress Press, 1998.

Otis, George, Jr. *The Twilight Labyrinth.* Grand Rapids: Chosen Books, 1997.

Perry, Troy. *The Lord Is My Shepherd And He Knows I'm Gay.* Austin, TX: Liberty Press, 1972.

Phillips, Anthony. *Ancient Israel's Criminal Law: A New Approach to the Decalogue.* New York: Schocken Books, 1970.

Philo. *On Joseph.*

Ringrose, Kathryn M. "Living In the Shadows: Eunuchs And Gender In Byzantium." Chap. 1 in *Third Sex, Third Gender: Beyond Sexual Dimorphism in Culture and History*, edited by Gilbert Herdt, 85-110, New York: Zone Books, 1993.

Scroggs, Robin. *The New Testament and Homosexuality.* Philadelphia: Fortress Press, 1983.

Stevenson, Walter. "Eunuchs and early Christianity." Chap. 7 in *Eunuchs In Antiquity And Beyond*, edited by Shaun Tougher, 143-160, London: Classical Press of Wales and Ducksworth, 2002.

Strong, James. *Strong's Exhaustive Concordance Of The Bible.* Nashville and New York: Abingdon Press, 1890.

Swaab, D. F. and E. Fliers. "A sexually dimorphic nucleus in the human brain." *Science* 228 (1985): 1112-1115.

Tompkins, Peter. *The Eunuch and the Virgin: A Study of Curious Customs*. New York: Clarkson N. Potter, 1962.

Tougher, Shaun F. "Byzantine Eunuchs: An Overview, with Special Reference To Their Creation And Origin." Chap. 8 in *Women, Men and Eunuchs: Gender in Byzantium*, edited by Liz James, 168-184, London and New York: Routledge, 1997.

_____. "In or Out? Origins of Court Eunuchs." Chap. 8 in *Eunuchs In Antiquity And Beyond*, edited by Shaun Tougher, 143-160, London: Classical Press of Wales and Ducksworth, 2002.

Unger, Merrill F. *Unger's Bible Dictionary,* 3rd ed. Chicago: Moody Press, 1966.

Wagner, C. Peter. *The ACTS of the HOLY SPIRIT Series: Spreading the Fire, Book 1, Acts 1- 8*. Ventura, CA: Regal Books, 1994.

_____. *The ACTS of the HOLY SPIRIT Series: Blazing the Way, Book 3, Acts 10- 15.*

Ventura, CA: Regal Books, 1995.

Watson, Alan, ed. *The Digest of Justinian*. Vol. 1, rev. ed. Philadelphia: University of Pennsylvania Press, 1988.

_____. *The Digest of Justinian*. Vol. 4. Philadelphia: University of Pennsylvania Press, 1985.

*Webster's New World Dictionary Of The American Language, College Edition*. Cleveland and New York: World, 1968.

Wenham, Gordon J. *Genesis 1-15*. Volume 1 of *Word Biblical Commentary*, David A. Hubbard and Glenn W. Barker, gen. eds. Nashville, Dallas, Mexico City, Rio De Janeiro, Beijing: Thomas Nelson, 1987.

Wilkerson, David. *America's Last Call: On the Brink Of A Financial Holocaust*. Lindale, TX: Wilkerson Trust Publications, 1998.

Young, Robert. *Young's Analytical Concordance To The Bible*. Grand Rapids: Eerdmans, 1991.

# ENDNOTES

1    "Timeline: Proposition 8," *Los Angeles Times*, June 23, 2010, accessed May 9, 2011, http://www.latimes.com/news/local/la-prop8-timeline,0,5431563.story?page=2.

2    John Schwartz, "California High Court Upholds Gay Marriage Ban, *New York Times,* May 26, 2009, accessed May 9, 2010, http://www.nytimes.com/2009/05/27/us/27marriage.html?_r=1&pagewanted=all.

3    "Prop. 8: Gay-marriage ban unconstitutional, court rules," *Los Angeles Times,* February 7, 2012, accessed May 25, 2012, http://latimesblogs.latimes.com/lanow/2012/02/gay-marriage-prop-8s-banruledunconstitutional.html.

4    Merriam-Webster Online Dictionary, s. v. "marriage," accessed May 8, 2010, Http://merriam-webster.com/dictionary/marriage.

5    David Kinnaman and Gabe Lyons, *Unchristian, What A New Generation Really Thinks About Christianity... And Why It Matters* (Grand Rapids: Baker Books, 2007), 97- 98.

6    Acts 10:9-47

7    Merriam-Webster Online Dictionary, s.v. "propaganda," accessed May 8, 2010, http://www.merriam-webster.com/dictionary/propaganda.

8    Merriam- Webster Online Dictionary, s. v. "agenda," accessed May 8, 2010, http://www.merriam-webster.com/dictionary/agenda.

9    *The Gay Agenda* is a 20 minute video produced by The Report in 1992. The producers are based out of the Spring Life Ministries Church in Lancaster, California. This is the same Church that re-ordained televangelist Jim Bakker in 1987.

10   Wayne Besen, *Anything But Straight: Unmasking the Scandals and Lies Behind the Ex-Gay Myth* (New York and London: Harrington Park Press, 2003), 113.

11   Merriam-Webster Online Dictionary, s. v. "propaganda," accessed May 10, 2010, http://merriam-webster.com/dictionary/propaganda.

12  Merriam-Webster Online Dictionary, s. v. "homophobia," accessed May 10, 2010, http://merriam-webster.com/dictionary/homophobia.

13  Besen, *Anything But Straight,* 16 and 22.

14  Ibid., 140.

15  Erik Eckholm, "Rift Forms in Movement as Belief in Gay "Cure" Is Renounced," *The New York Times,* July 6, 2012, accessed July 10, 2012, http://www.nytimes.com/2012/07/07/us/a-leaders-renunciation-of-ex-gay-tenets-causes-a-schism.html.

16  Neil Katz, "Schools Battle Suicide Surge, Anti-Gay Bullying," *CBS News,* October 11, 2010, accessed June 6, 2011, http://www.cbsnews.com/8301-504763_162-20019163-10391704.html.

17  Peggy O'Hare, "Parents say bullies drove their son to take his life," Houston Chronicle, September 27, 2010, accessed June 7, 2011, http://www.chron.com/disp/story.mpl/metropolitan/7220896.html.

18  Jeannie Kever, "Sunday is Bring Your Gay Teen to Church Day," *Houston Chronicle,* February 19, 2011, accessed May 16, 2012, http://www.chron.com/life/houston-belief/article/Sunday-is-Bring-Your-Gay-Teen-to-Church-Day-1692825.php.

19  A. Bertocci, "Jerry Falwell Dies at Age 73, *Yahoo! Voices,* May 17, 2007, accessed May 9, 2010, http://voices.yahoo.com/jerry-falwell-dies-age-73-346212.html.

20  David Wilkerson, *America's Last Call: On the Brink of a Financial Holocaust* (Lindale, TX: Wilkerson Trust Publications, 1998), 54.

21  Francis Frangipane, *This Day We Fight!: Breaking The Bondage Of A Passive Spirit* (Grand Rapids: Chosen Books, 2005), 31.

22  Kinnaman, *Unchristian,* 92.

23  1 Cor. 13:8.

24  1 John 4:16-18.

25  For more information on Teach Ministries and Mary Lou Wallner's story see Wallner's book *The Slow Miracle of Transformation* and http://www.teach-ministries.org/main.html

26  Vern Bullough, *Sexual Variance in Society and History* (Chicago and London: University of Chicago Press, 1976), 637.

27  Robin Scroggs, *The New Testament and Homosexuality* (Philadelphia: Fortress Press, 1983), 63.

28  Jim Kepner, *Becoming A People... a 4,000 year gay and lesbian chronology* (Hollywood, CA: National Gay Archives, 1983), 9.

29   Ibid., 18.

30   James Strong, *Strong's Exhaustive Concordance of the Bible* (Nashville and New York: Abingdon Press, 1890), 6942 qadash.

31   Ibid., 6945, qadesh.

32   Ibid.

33   2 Kings 23:4-20 and 1 Kings 15:12-13.

34   Deut. 23:18-19 (New King James Version) and *Strong's,* 6948 qedeshah, 6945 qadesh, 2181 zanah, and 3611 keleb.

35   David Greenberg, *The Construction of Homosexuality* (Chicago and London: University of Chicago, 1988), 95.

36   Ibid.

37   John Boswell, *Christianity, Social Tolerance and Homosexuality* (Chicago and London: University of Chicago Press, 1980), 82.

38   L. Robert Arthur, *The Sex Texts: Sexuality, Gender and Relationships in the Bible* (Omaha, NE: Arthur, 1994), 86-87.

39   Martti Nissinen, *Homoeroticism in the Biblical World: A Historical Perspective,* trans. Kirsi Stjerna (Minneapolis: Fortress Press, 1998), 12.

40   Bernadette, Brooten, *Love Between Women: Early Christian Responses To Female Homoeroticism* (Chicago and London: University of Chicago Press, 1996), 3.

41   See Matt. 8:5-13 and Luke 7:1-10.

42   Donald Mader, "The Entimos Pais of Matthew 8:5-13 and Luke 7:1-10," in *Homosexuality and Religion and Philosophy,* ed. Wayne R. Dynes (New York: Garland, 1992), 226-235. Mader's views on "pais" are supported by K. J. Dover in *Greek Homosexuality* (Cambridge: Harvard University Press, 1978).

43   Strong, *Strong's,* 1784 entimos.

44   Matt. 19:12 (NKJV).

45   Matt. 19:11 (NKJV).

46   There are various studies on the word "entimos" used in Luke's text to describe the intimate servant lover of the Centurion. Apparently, Jesus had no issue with the Centurion nor with his lover and was willing to heal him. See Luke 7 and Matt. 8. Also, see my position on Jesus' Sodom and Gomorrah reference in Luke 17 in Chapter 8 and my position on Jesus' reference to *malakos* in Chapter 9.

47   I would like to give credit to John J. McNeill in *The Church and the Homosexual* (1976) for first encouraging me in this direction regarding the meaning of the word

*eunuch* in Jesus' comment on born eunuchs. Also, more recently, I would like to credit Faris Malik for his unpublished work called *"Born Eunuchs: Homosexual Identity in the Ancient World."* For further information on Malik's research which focuses on born eunuchs as the equivalent of gay males today, see http://www. well.com/user/aqarius/thesis.htm.

48  Robert Young, *Young's Analytical Concordance To The Bible* (Grand Rapids: WM. B. Eerdmans, 1991), 308. References to *eunouchos* are Matt. 19:12 twice; and Acts 8:27, 8:34, 8:36, 8:38 and 8:39.

49  Young, *Young's Analytical,* 309. The term *eunouchizo* is found twice in Matt. 19:12.

50  Strong, *Strong's,* 2135 eunouchos.

51  Ibid., 153, 308 and 712 for *saris* and 791 for *Rabsaris.* References to *saris* are on 153 listed under *chamberlain* as 2 Kings 23:11; Esther 1:10, 1:12, 1:15, 2:3, 2:14, 2:15, 2:21, 4:4, 4:5, 6:2, 6:14, and 7:9. References to *saris* on 308 as *eunuch* are 2 Kings 9:32, 20:18; Isa. 39:7, 56:3, and 56:4; Jer. 29:2, 34:19, 38:7, 41:16, and 52:25; Dan. 1 1:3, 1:7, 1:8, 1:9, 1:10, 1:11 and 1:18. References to *saris* on 712 as *eunuch* is Gen. 37:36, 39:1, 40:2, and 40:7; 1 Sam. 8:15; 1 Kings 22:9; 2 Kings 8:6, 24:12, 24:15, and 25:19; 1 Chron. 28:1; and 2 Chron. 18:8. Finally, references to *Rabsaris* are Jer. 39:3 and 39:13 and then 2 Kings 18:17.

52  Strong, *Strong's,* 5631 saris.

53  2 Kings 18:17 and Jer. 39:3 and 13.

54  Strong, *Strong's,* 7227 rab.

55  The British Museum, "Important Breakthrough In Biblical Archeology," http://www.britishmuseum.org/the_museum/news_and_press?releases/press_ releases/2007/biblical?archeology?find.aspx (accessed May 9, 2010).

56  Faris Malik in "Born Eunuchs" first led me to sources on eunuchs in the Roman Law, the Talmud, and by early Church Fathers. Rick Brentlinger has a more recent treatment of these same sources in *Gay Christian 101.*

57  *The Digest of Justinian,* vol. 4. (Philadelphia: University of Pennsylvania Press, 1985), 944.

58  *The Digest of Justinian*, vol. 1., rev. ed. (Philadelphia: University of Pennsylvania Press, 1998), 128.

59  Come and Hear, "Babylonian Talmud: Tractate Yebamoth, Folio 80b," Jew's College/Soncino English Translation of the Babylonian Talmud, http://www. come-and-hear.com/yebamoth/yebamoth_80.html (accessed May 4, 2010).

60  Ibid.

61  Arthur, *Sex Texts,* 90.

62  Brooten, *Love Between Women,* 69.

63   Ibid., 133.

64   L. Robert Arthur in *Sex Texts* and Faris Malik in his unpublished work entitled "Born Eunuchs: Homosexual Identity in the Ancient World" first introduced me to these apocryphal writings.

65   Clement of Alexandria, *Paedagogus,* 3.4., in Clement of Alexandria: Christ The Educator, trans. Simon P. Wood. (New York: Fathers of the Church, 1954), 221.

66   Clement of Alexandria, *The Stromata,* 3.1.1. John Ernest Leonard Oulton and Henry Chadwick, eds. (Philadelphia: Westminster Press, 1954), 40.

67   The Apostolic Canons, "Canon 21," The Saint Pachomius Library, http://www.voskrese.info/spl/aposcanon.html (accessed May 4, 2010).

68   Gregory of Nazianzus, *Oration* 37. 16-17., in A Select Library of Nicene And Post-Nicene Fathers of The Christian Church, vol. 7. Philip Schaff and Henry Wace, eds. (New York: Christian Literature , 1894), 342.

69   Gregory of Nazianzus, *Oration* 37.19., in A Select Library of Nicene And Post-Nicene Fathers of The Christian Church, vol. 7. Philip Schaff and Henry Wace, eds. (New York: Christian Literature , 1894), 343.

70   Ps. 107:39.

71   Greenberg, *Construction of Homosexuality,* 123.

72   Peter Tompkins, *The Eunuch and the Virgin: A Study of Curious Customs* (New York: Clarkson N. Potter, 1962), 14.

73   Ibid., 31.

74   Ibid., 16.

75   Ibid.

76   Greenberg, *Construction of Homosexuality*, 121. See Herodotus 1.135.

77   Isa. 39:7.

78   Greenberg, *Construction of Homosexuality,* 122.

79   Ibid., 123.

80   Allen Edwardes, *Erotica Judaica: A Sexual History of the Jews* (New York: Julian Press, 1967), 103-105.

81   Greenberg, *Construction of Homosexuality*, 121.

82   Taisuke Mitamura, *Chinese Eunuchs: The Structure Of Intimate Politics,* trans. Charles A. Pomeroy. (Ruland, VT and Tokyo: Charles E. Tuttle, 1963), 28-29.

83   Ibid., 127.

84   Ibid., 27-28.

85   Tompkins, *Eunuch and the Virgin,* 31-33.

86   Ibid., 37.

87   Mitamura, *Chinese Eunuchs*, 49.

88   Shaun F. Tougher, "Byzantine Eunuchs: An Overview, with Special Reference To Their Creation And Origin." in *Women, Men and Eunuchs: Gender in Byzantium,* ed. Liz James (London and New York: Routledge, 1997), 171.

89   Tompkins, *Eunuch and the Virgin*, 15.

90   Mitamura, *Chinese Eunuchs*, 32.

91   Ibid., 27.

92   Ibid., 21.

93   Tougher, *Byzantine Eunuchs*, 177.

94   Serena Nanda, *Neither Man nor Woman: The Hijras of India* (Belmont, CA: Wadsworth , 1990), xiii.

95   See Esther 2:3, 2:15, 4:4, and 4:5; Gen. 37:36, Gen. 39:1, 40:2 and 40:7; Dan. l:3, 1:7-11 and 1:18.

96   Early Christian Writings, The Works of Philo Judaeus, On Joseph, 12, http://www.earlychristianwritings.com/yonge/book23.html (accessed May 7, 2010).

97   1 Sam. 8:15 (NRSV). (Brackets mine for eunuch or saris.)

98   2 Kings 9:32.

99   2 Kings 8:6.

100  Jer. 38:7.

101  Jer. 52:25 and 2 Kings 25:19.

102  I want to acknowledge that I was encouraged to study all the *saris* and *eunuch* references in the Scriptures only after being introduced to Faris Malik's unpublished work "Born Eunuchs: Homosexual Identity in the Ancient World" back in 1999. It was then that I discovered the Biblical references to non-castrated eunuchs who were favored by God and in covenant with God. The discovery of these natural eunuchs in 1 Chronicles 28:1, 2 kings 23:11, Jeremiah 34:19, Jeremiah 29:1-2 and Acts 8:27-39 is of paramount importance.

103  1 Chron. 28:1. (Brackets mine from *Strong's*, 5631 saris.).

104    2 Kings 20:18 and Isa. 39:7.

105    Deut. 23:1 (King James Version).

106    Lev. 21:20 (KJV).

107    Strong, *Strong's*, 6945 qadesh.

108    2 Kings 23:11. (Brackets mine from *Strong's*, 5631 saris.).

109    Strong, *Strong's*, 5414 Nathan.

110    Ibid., For Melech, 4427 Malak is Hebrew root word of 4428 Melek.

111    Ibid., 5419 Nathan-Melech.

112    Jer. 34:19-20 (KJV). (Brackets mine from *Strong's*, 5631 saris.).

113    Jer. 29:1-2. (Brackets mine from *Strong's*, 5631 saris.).

114    Strong, *Strong's*, 3629 kilyah.

115    D. Guthrie and others, eds., *The New Bible Commentary Revised* (Grand Rapids: WM. B. Eerdsmans, 1970), 539.

116    Ibid., 3372 yare from Ps. 139:14 translated as *fearfully* in the NIV and KJV.

117    Ibid., 6395 palah from Ps. 139:14 translated as *wonderfully* in the NIV and KJV.

118    Matt. 19:12 (NKJV).

119    Lynne Yamaguchi Fletcher, *The First Gay Pope and other records* (Boston: Alyson Publications, 1992), 28. Aristotle's life spanned 384-322 BC.

120    John P. De Cecco and David Allen Parker, eds. "The Biology of Homosexuality: Sexual Orientation or Sexual Preference?" in *Sex, Cells, and Same-Sex Desire: The Biology of Sexual Preference* (New York: Harrington Park Press, 1995), 2.

121    Myers, *Exploring Psychology,* 398.

122    Ibid. (For more information see S. LeVay, "A difference in hypothalamic structure between heterosexual and homosexual men," *Science* 253 (1991), 1034-1037.).

123    D. F. Swaab and E. Fliers, "A sexually dimorphic nucleus in the human brain," *Science* 228 (1985), 1112-1115.

124    De Cecco, *Biology of Homosexuality,* 4.

125    Myers, *Exploring Psychology,* 398.

126    De Cecco, *Biology of Homosexuality,* 6. (For more information see D. H. Hamer, S. Hu, V. L. Magnuson, N. Hu, & A. M. L. Pattatucci, "A linkage between DNA markers on the X chromosome and male sexual orientation," *Science* 261 (1993), 321-327.).

127    Brian S. Mustanski, et al., "A genomewide scan of male sexual orientation," *Human Genetics,* 116 no. 4, (2005), 272.

128    Ibid., 278.

129    Lee Ellis and M. Ashley Ames, "Neurohormonal functioning and sexual orientation: A theory of homosexuality- heterosexuality," *Psychological Bulletin* 101, no. 2 (1987), 233-258.

130    Ibid., 248.

131    R. Blanchard R. and A. F. Bogaert, A. F. "Homosexuality in men and the number of older brothers," *American Journal of Psychiatry* 153 (1996), 28.

132    R. Blanchard and Lee Ellis, "Birth weight, sexual orientation and the sex of preceding siblings," *Journal of Biosocial Science,* 33 (2001), 460.

133    R. Blanchard, and J. M. Cantor, A. F. Bogaert, S. M. Breedlove and L. Ellis, "Interaction of fraternal birth order and handedness in the development of male homosexuality," *Hormones and Behavior* 49 (2006), 409.

134    Myers, *Exploring Psychology*, 400.

135    Ibid.

136    David Crary, "Psychologists repudiate gay-to-straight therapy," *Associated Press*, August 5, 2009, accessed May 9, 2010, http://news.yahoo.com/s/ap/20090805/ap_on_re_us_psychologists_gays.

137    "Vatican Science Panel Told By Pope: Galileo Was Right," *New York Times*, November 1, 1992, accessed May 20, 2010, http://www.nytimes.com/1992/11/01/world/vatican-science-panel-told-by-pope-galileo-was-right.html. John Paul II apologizes for treatment of Galileo in address to the Pontifical Academy of Sciences on November 1, 1992.

138    Isa. 56:4-5 (NKJV).

139    Strong, *Strong's*, 3037 yad.

140    Blue Letter Bible, "Gesenius's Lexicon for "place" (Strong's 3037, yad) in Isaiah 56:5," Gesenius's Lexicon, http://www.blueletterbible.org/lang/lexicon/lexicon.cfm?Strongs=H3027&t=KJV (accessed May 10, 2010).

141    Strong, *Strong's,* 2896 towb.

142    Ibid.

143   See John 13:23-25, John 19:26-27, John 20:2-10, John 21:5-7, and John 21:20.

144   John 14:26 and John 16:13.

145   2 Cor. 3:17.

146   Webster's Online Dictionary, s. v. "lie," accessed May 9, 2010, http://www. websters-online-dictionary.org/definitions/lie..

147   John 8:44.

148   Merrill Unger, *Unger's Bible Dictionary,* 3rd ed. (Chicago: Moody Press, 1957), s.v. "sodomite."

149   See Luke 10:10-12.

150   Strong, *Strong's,* 3045 yada.

151   Maria Hinojosa, "NYC Officer Arrested In Alleged Sexual Attack On Suspect," *CNN U.S.,* August 14, 1997, accessed May 9, 2010,     http://articles.cnn. com/1997-08-14/us/9708_14_police.torture_1_police-officers-70th-precinct-thomas-bruder?_s=PM:US.

152   Strong, *Strong's,* 8441 to`ebah.

153   Scroggs, *New Testament And Homosexuality,* 80.

154   Greenberg, *Construction of Homosexuality,* 201.

155   Nissinen, *Homoeroticism,* 89.

156   Ibid.

157   Boswell, *Christianity,* 97-98.

158   Leon Morris, *Luke: An Introduction And Commentary,* Tyndale New Testament Commentaries (Illinois and England: Intervarsity Press, 1974 and 1988), 286. Bible translators deal with Luke 17:34 in various ways because the word "*men*" is not included in the original Greek text. The Tyndale New Testament Commentary by Leon Morris states that the original Greek text does use the masculine gender in both "*one*" and "*the other.*" The traditional reading of Greek would mean that the phrase should be read "*two men in one bed*" as the King James Version of the Bible translates it. It is interesting that other translators remove the word "men" or just omit the verse completely. Leon Morris concludes that it could mean man and wife however. The Interpreter's Bible Commentary for the Gospel of Luke and the Gospel of John, Volume VIII, (1952) states on page 304 that "Two in vs. 34 probably means two men, as alternative illustration to two (women) in vs. 35; but the earlier two could mean man and wife." I don't think there would be any question as to how to interpret this verse if the subject was not about two men in bed together.

159   Lev. 18:22 (NKJV).

160    Lev. 20:13 (NKJV).

161    B. Z. Goldberg, *The Sacred Fire* (New York: Garden City, 1930) 186.

162    Strong, *Strong's,* 2233 zera.

163    Blue Letter Bible, "Gesenius's Lexicon for "seed" (Strong's H-2233, zera) in Leviticus 18:21," http://www.blueletterbible.org/lang/lexicon/lexicon. cfm?Strongs=H2233&t=KJV (accessed May 9, 2011). Gesenius's Lexicon compares *zera* in Leviticus 18:21 to how it is used in Leviticus 15:16 confirming that the meaning in 18:21 is sexual relations or the passing of seed to another person in sexual relations.

164    Arthur, *Sex Texts,* 78.

165    Strong, *Strong's,* 8441 to`ebah.

166    Anthony Phillips, *Ancient Israel's Criminal Law: A New Approach to the Decalogue* (New York: Schocken Books, 1970), 121-122.

167    Deut. 7:25-26. (Brackets mine of *Strong's,* 8441 to`ebah.).

168    Jer. 2:7 and 11. (Brackets mine of *Strong's*, 8441 to`ebah.).

169    Mal. 2:11. (Brackets mine of *Strong's*, 8441 to`ebah.).

170    Boswell, *Christianity,* 100.

171    Strong, *Strong's,* 6942 qadash.

172    Ibid., 6945 qadesh.

173    1 Kings 15:12. (Brackets mine of *Strong's,* 6945 qadash.).

174    1 Kings 22:46. (Brackets mine of *Strong's*, 6954 qadash.).

175    2 Kings 23:7. (Brackets mine of *Strong's*, 6945 qadash.).

176    Goldberg, *Sacred Fire,* 186-187.

177    Greenberg, *Construction of Homosexuality,* 106.

178    Ibid., 96-97.

179    Nissinen, *Homoeroticism,* 42-43.

180    Greenberg, *Construction of Homosexuality,* 106.

181    Luke 24:45.

182    1 Cor. 6:9-10. (Brackets mine.).

183    1 Tim. 1:9-11. (Brackets mine.).

184    Boswell, *Christianity,* 341.

185    Nissinen, *Homoeroticism,* 116.

186    C. Peter Wagner, *The ACTS of the Holy Spirit Series: Blazing the Way, Book 3, Acts 15-28* (Ventura, CA: Regal Books, 1995), 123.

187    Everett Ferguson, *Backgrounds of Early Christianity,* 2nd ed. (Grand Rapids: WM. B. Eerdmans , 1993), 260.

188    Ralph Blair, *Homosexualities, Faith, Facts and Fairy Tales* (New York: Blair, 1991), 19.

189    Greenberg, *Construction of Homosexuality,* 98.

190    Catherine Kroeger, "The Apostle Paul and the Greco-Roman Cults of Women," *Journal of the Evangelical Society* 30 (March 1987), 37.

191    Boswell, *Christianity,* 352-353.

192    Dale Martin, "Arsenokoites and Malakos: Meanings and Consequences," in *Biblical Ethics & Homosexuality: Listening to Scripture*, ed. Robert L. Brawley (Kentucky: Westminster John Knox Press, 1996), 120.

193    Scroggs, *New Testament And Homosexuality,* 120.

194    Martin, *Arsenokoites and Malakos,* 118.

195    Boswell, *Christianity,* 106.

196    Ibid., 107.

197    Nissinen, *Homoeroticism,* 117.

198    Boswell, *Christianity,* 339.

199    Martin, *Arsenokoites and Malakos,* 125.

200    Matt. 11:8 and Luke 7:25.

201    Matt. 11:7-9. (Brackets mine.).

202    For more information on Herod's eunuch servants see Josephus' Antiquities of the Jews 16:8.1-5.

203    Geoffrey Bromiley, *Theological Dictionary Of The New Testament* (Grand Rapids: WM. B. Eerdsmans Publishing Company, 1985), s.vv. "latreuein, sebazomai." See both entries for phrase "worshiped and served" in Romans 1:25 at 503-504 and 1010.

204   Ferguson, *Backgrounds,* 264-265.

205   Greenberg, *Construction of Homosexuality,* 98.

206   Goldberg, *Sacred Fire,* 176-177 and Ferguson, *Backgrounds*, 264.

207   Boswell, *Christianity,* 111.

208   Ibid., 110.

209   Goldberg, *Sacred Fire,* 172-173.

210   Arthur, *Sex Texts,* 86-87.

211   Strong, *Strong's,* 2134, eunouchizo.

212   Greenburg, *Construction of Homosexuality,* 223 and 224.

213   Ibid., 224.

214   First Council of Nicaea- 321 AD, "Canon 1," St. Michael's Depot, http://www. piar.hu/councils/ecum01.htm (accessed May 5, 2010).

215   Greenburg, *Construction of Homosexuality,* 223 and 224.

216   Strong, *Strong's,* 5486 charisma, is a gift of grace, a free gift, divine gratuity, spiritual endowment, miraculous faculty.

217   Strong, *Strong's,* 5663 Ebed Melek.

218   Strong, *Strong's,* 5419 Nathan-Melech.

219   Strong, *Strong's,* 5414 Nathan.

220   Strong, *Strong's,* 4428 Melech.

221   Strong, *Strong's,* 4427 Malak.

222   Acts 8:27.

223   C. Peter Wagner, *The ACTS of the Holy Spirit Series: Spreading the Fire, Book 1, Acts 1-8* (Ventura, CA: Regal Books, 1994), 37. The Lausanne Committee For World Evangelization agreed upon this definition for "people group."

224   *Webster's New World Dictionary Of The American Language,* College Ed., s.v. "nation."

225   John Dawson, *Healing America's Wounds* (Ventura, CA: Regal Books, 1994), 24.

226   Ibid., 120-121.

227   Troy Perry, *The Lord Is My Shepherd And He Knows I'm Gay* (Austin, TX: Liberty Press, 1972), 108.

228   Riazat Butt, "Gene Robinson goes but rift remains: Strain proves too much for gay bishop," *The Guardian,* November 7, 2010, accessed May 8, 2011, http://www.guardian.co.uk/world/2010/nov/07/gene-robinson-anglican-us-episcopal.html.

229   Glbtq Social Sciences, "Stonewall Riots," http://glbtq.com/social-sciences/stonewall_riots.html (accessed May 20, 2011).

230   Adelle M. Banks, "Study: Youth see Christians as judgmental, anti-gay," *USA Today*, October 10, 2007, accessed May 7, 2012, http://www.usatoday.com/news/religion/2007-10-10-christians-young_N.htm. Interview with David Kinnaman, president of the Barna Research Group on his recent book *Unchristian.*

231   Ibid.

232   The Auto Illustrator, "Evangelism," Sermon Illustrations, http://www.autoillustrator.com/online, (accessed May 9, 2010).

233   Matt. 16:18.

234   John 2:16.

235   Mark 11:17.

236   John 1:14.

237   Mary Bruce, "Obama Talks Gay Marriage, Politics, and Pop Culture on 'The View,'" *ABC News,* May 15, 2012, accessed May 17, 2012, http://abcnews.go.com/Politics/OTUS/obama-talks-gay-marriage-politics-pop-culture-view/story?id=16350683.

238   Unger, *Unger's Bible Dictionary*, s.v. "marriage."

239   See 2 Sam. 12:8 where God's word to David through Nathan the prophet is it was God who gave David wives.

240   Richard Brentlinger, *Gay Christian 101: Spiritual Self-Defense For Gay Christians* (Pace, FL: Salient Press, 2007), 21-26.

Whether you want to purchase bulk copies of
*God's Gay Agenda*
or buy another book for a friend, get it now at:
**www.glorytabernacle.com**

**If you have a book that you would like to publish**,
contact Jon McHatton, Publisher,
at (480) 332-9139 or email: jon@abooksmind.com